Endorsemen

Insightful and profoundly practical. This book contains essential keys that all of us need to successfully walk out our marketplace engagement daily.

Daniel Lim, CEO
International House of Prayer
ihopkc.org

———

Impact Your Sphere of Influence is a great read. As President and CEO of Fellowship of Companies for Christ International (FCCI) we believe that He calls business leaders to participate in the building of His kingdom through our business. I pray that this book encourages and equips many for works of service.

Terence Chatmon, President & CEO
FCCI
www.fcci.org

———

In reading this book, expect to impact your sphere of influence. Not only will you learn the principles but also the practical ways you can bring God's presence to the marketplace.

Luis Bush, Servant
Transform World 2020
www.transform-world.net

Impact Your Sphere of Influence will challenge you to view your life and employment from God's perspective enabling you to find their meaning, purpose, and sacredness for which everyone longs. The pearls of wisdom that Linda Fields unearths in these pages will prove to be priceless.

Dusty Kemp, Pastor
New Life Church, Houston, TX
www.newlifechurch.net

_____

With all the talk of taking the mountains of influence in the marketplace, few are stressing the importance learned from one mountain climber and world changer, Moses, who said, "If Thy presence does not go with us, do not lead us up from here." Going "up from here" into workplace leadership, promotions, etc, without God's presence, has led to more workplace stress and family issues at home as Christian leaders in the marketplace come under the sway to the ways of their "mountain" or marketplace environment—instead of influencing it with the peace and wisdom that comes from having fellowship in God's presence. This book is a "right now" word in your pursuit of carrying God's presence unto workplace excellence.

William Ford III
Director of Marketplace Leadership
Christ For The Nations Institute
cfni.org
willfordministries.com

In Linda Fields' new book *Impact Your Sphere Of Influence* she invites the reader to a very personal journey – it's her own journey. This inspiring book details how she combined the two worlds of Ministry and Marketplace with great success. Many believers see this as two totally separate entities - Linda shares openly that it is one and the same. If you are in the marketplace or even thinking of jumping into the business world - this book is for you. It will encourage you, and give you skillful instruction in the day-to-day world of the marketplace. You too can bring His presence to the office, into every meeting and impact your sphere of Influence.

Julie Meyer
International House Of Prayer –KC
Juliemeyer.com

Beautiful. Linda unveils the keys to being the light of the world. As we put to practice the principles in Linda's *Impact Your Sphere of Influence,* the world will taste and see that God is good! She reveals the wisdom to equip believers so that others see Jesus.

Saleim Kahleh, Muslim found by Jesus
SKministries.org
Associate University Minister
Houston Baptist University

LINDA FIELDS

IMPACT
Your Sphere of
INFLUENCE

BRINGING GOD'S PRESENCE
TO THE WORKPLACE

LINDA FIELDS

v

Additional orders and Author Contact: lindafields@7M-pact.com

ISBN-13: 978-0983480075

Fields Enterprise Solutions

Printed in the United States

DEDICATION

TO THE LORD MOST HOLY
May we know You better.

"But the people who know their God
shall be strong,
and carry out *great exploits*.
And those of the people who understand
shall instruct many."
Daniel 11:32b-33a

IMPACT Your Sphere of INFLUENCE

CONTENTS

IMPACT Your Sphere of INFLUENCE

FOREWORD by Mike Bickle

Director, International House of Prayer

Kansas City, Missouri

I have observed over the last 30 years that there is an increasing cry to understand and fulfill the spiritual calling of believers in the marketplace. There is a question that lurks in the heart of men and women in the workplace on Monday mornings that must be addressed: "Am I really doing work that matters to God?" It gnaws at many as they make their commute and attend meetings, whether they love their job or just endure it, waiting for the weekend. Over the past 10 years this cry has grown louder and louder. Why is this?

Regretfully, it is because of a lingering misconception concerning what ministry really is. We have failed to see that ministry is in fact fulfilling *any* assignment that the Lord has given us: in the Church or full-time ministry org chart, the mission field, the workplace, the government, the home or as a university student.

Historically the error has been a lack of recognition that from the Lord's perspective, there is no difference in importance between those who are on the front lines at mechanic shops, banks, and talent agencies and those who office in church buildings or make their way evangelizing in Algeria.

The main point of this book is to resolve this dilemma. You must settle your life calling. The Lord has placed you in an assignment in society by His design. The job assignments you do are avenues where you express your life calling.

There is not a more favored status for preachers, missionaries, or those in full-time ministry. Everyone's work is important to the Lord as they labor in God's will regardless of the sphere of influence—Media, Government, Family, Celebration, Religion, Education, and Economy—all have the same invitation to devote themselves to knowing the Lord and doing His will.

Pastors and teachers in the body of Christ must clearly proclaim the message that there is no difference in importance or prestige in God's eyes in the diverse ministry assignments that He gives His people. The key is to do God's will regardless of where He has placed us.

Consider how the Father observed Jesus' everyday life and activities. Jesus sweating with hammer in hand in Joseph's carpenter shop, Jesus conversing with the woman at the well, Jesus preaching in the synagogue, and Jesus helping the fishermen—each instance carried the same worth. Everything Jesus did counted because it was designed by and done in partnership with the Father. The same is now true for us because there's a seamless reality of life, flowing from the Holy Spirit in us, expressed as we go about our jobs and build up our cities and communities.

It's time for pastors and teachers in the body of Christ to address the lie that has hindered many who work in schools, at city hall, or at news stations. It's time to bless what these marketplace men and women have been doing and help His people connect with the Lord's purposes in their life. That is what *Impact Your Sphere of Influence* does.

In reading this book, I believe you will become powerfully validated that your occupation really matters to God and is holy as you devote it to Him. You will enjoy identifying ways you can release the presence of God in the workplace. I pray that many of you gain a new measure of clarity and confidence about the Lord's purposes in your various spheres of society and authority.

Linda has assembled a body of work which will not only inform you but beckon you to get on track with a plan to make your sense of calling doable. I encourage the reader to engage with the process and reach for the fellowship it requires to move into your impact. This is your safety—to go with a team of friends, like Jesus.

The Lord calls His people to be great in His eyes by embracing a lifestyle of faithful obedience to His will (Mt. 5:19). We are not to repent of our desire for greatness; we are only to repent of pursuing it in a wrong way.

I invite you to pray a crucial prayer as you walk through this book. From Ephesians 1:17-18, ask the Lord for grace to know the hope of your calling or your assignment from Him in the various seasons of your life. You are not just a paycheck for the church to collect. You are a leader in the kingdom and this book will strengthen your sense of calling. Dive into this book with that in mind. It will bring dignity to what you are doing every single day of your life.

Linda Fields leads 7M-pact, a ministry to those in the marketplace. This ministry is a part of the International House of Prayer family of Kansas City. She brings decades of corporate experience and success with much practical insight along with years of engaging with Jesus in her prayer life. She has done a superb job of combining a genuine spirituality, which includes discerning and applying God's wisdom in the marketplace, with a life of faithful obedience to Jesus; she has done this in the context of a growing prayer life.

I highly recommend Linda and this book.

ACKNOWLEDGMENTS

Thank you Holly Fields, Jane Harris, Jackie McLeod, Jackie Macgirvin, Reagan Loughry, Mike De Vincenzi…And a host of encouragers in The Joseph Co team, the Move Forward affiliate group, and my Board for your help, your editing, your insights, and your prayers and belief that I could complete this work. Thank you for listening, giving feedback, helping me wade through five years worth of processing on this valuable subject to emerge with clarity that we are in fact designed to bring impact in our spheres of influence, each and every one of us.

I loved the process along side each of you. A clear message of hope for every man and woman in the marketplace doing valuable work for God resounds on each page of every chapter. I love the product and cannot wait to hear the stories of the readers who grasp a vision beyond the drone of busy life to step into their sacred calls in the marketplace.

Rick Fields, I absolutely love you and cannot imagine any other person being all that you are to me.

TO THE READER

For every believer in the workplace who has wrestled with the question of whether they should quit their job to go into full-time ministry, or wondered if there was spiritual value to working in other spheres of society, I offer my own journey as an answer to that question. Because I value learning and have learned exhilarating things about life in the workplace, I have also documented the processes I have developed along the way.

I am writing this as though we are meeting together in a coffee shop having a long conversation about important things regarding your calling and career track. My writing is my personal story, my research, and my process; I pray this work will be a precise tool that empowers you to fulfill your own destiny.

Like the Apostle John writes in I John 1:1-3, I can only speak of what I have seen with my eyes, what I have handled and experienced concerning the Word of Life and how it is manifested in work – hence my relational approach to sharing experiences as I sit down at the table with you, coffee in hand. Also like John, I pray it increases your fellowship with like-minded believers and with the Father, the Holy Spirit, and with Jesus Himself. I pray that your joy is made full as you recognize your vocation for what it is meant to be.

Throughout the book, I have marked action points or key observations as follows:

➜ **KEY:** Take note when you come to the Keys.

As my gift, download your companion 90-Day Personal Prayer Guide at lindafields.org, then grab your coffee or tea, and let's begin.

Linda Fields

Chapter 1
The Invitation: You Are Invited to Engage with the Holy at Work

[9] What profit has the worker from that in which he labors? [10] I have seen the God-given task with which the sons of men are to be occupied. [11] He has made everything beautiful in its time. Also He has put eternity in their hearts, except that no one can find out the work that God does from beginning to end. [12] I know that nothing is better for them than to rejoice, and to do good in their lives, [13] and also that every man should eat and drink and enjoy the good of all his labor—it is the gift of God. (Eccl. 3:9-13) NKJV[2]

The Conflict within Our Souls

Can it be that a man or woman in the workplace who is available to God may synergistically partner with Him in his or her professional life, bringing results from heaven to earth?

One of my clients wrote me this message after I had taken the opportunity during a meeting to pray for a member of our team who was facing some serious health problems.

LINDA FIELDS

"Linda, what a refreshing pleasure to see the spiritual and the workplace come together. Thank you for praying for Claude in our business meeting today."

Why do so many people struggle to find spiritual significance in their professional lives? Is it true that spiritual 'work' is only to be done by those in full-time religious roles such as preachers, missionaries and professional church staff? Marketplace Christians have accepted a confining definition of work which strips us of the expectation that we will bring God's presence to those we encounter through our jobs. It is no wonder there is so much dissatisfaction in the workplace. Waiting for the weekend, counting down the days to retirement and marking time have replaced flourishing, thriving careers where engaged Leader-Believers set the standards for excellence and enjoy their work.

→**KEY**: It's time for Leader-Believers to step into
their true identity.

The term "Leader-Believer" describes the man or woman who partners with God in all arenas of life in such a way that they are becoming more like Jesus and impacting those around them. When believers step into leadership, things begin to happen and to change in us and around us. We then influence others, benefitting our communities. Often we are not even aware of our effect because it is second nature. Your leadership will cause others to want to join you in some way, regardless of your rank and title. Leader-Believers create lasting impact as janitors, receptionists, and CEOs. Everyone has an on-ramp to leadership as a believer.

Observation indicates that a large percentage of people today are feeling a great desire to do things that count for eternity, regardless of their spiritual affiliation. Social justice movements are growing and people are searching for meaningful ways to do good things. The Bible says that all of us "have eternity set in our hearts" (Eccl. 3:11), yet in the time it takes to find our niche and become educated and skilled in a profession, the exhilaration which we once felt about our chosen field has waned; we subtly or not so subtly get the message that the real spiritual work of Christianity is done by the clergy – those in full-time religious work.

In fact, we begin to feel cheated of making a meaningful contribution because we're now less than those who have chosen full-time ministry work. We are "of the world," we're not even sure we should be earning a paycheck (is that holy?), and if we do it must be solely for the purpose of funding *real* ministry and the really good guys and gals who go to Africa. These are the ones who are doing truly wonderful work, perhaps with orphans or the Peace Corps. The fact that they have traveled to another country offers instant credibility to the work they are doing. We feel we must prove to them we are also doing honorable work.

So no matter how many times we try to justify our career choices by reading about Paul's missionary journeys and how he supported himself making tents, we still have this haunting feeling we've chosen a less desirable path as a bookkeeper, doctor, lawyer, teacher, businessman, politician, or I dare say, a media or entertainment professional. We calm ourselves by remembering that our sole purpose is to make money to give to those who are doing the really important work.

The problem is that day in and day out, God made us to flourish in our calling, and without proper perspective on the glory and dignity of our job assignment, we're left to a meaningless work week. No matter how hard we try to imagine that our marketing company or legal services are really helping to advance Christianity, we're not empowered in our own sphere of influence to engage the aching humanity around us looking for a little church service right where we are – in the marketplace or our place of work.

A Holy Professional Story

God has created us to impact the world and engage in
meaningful endeavor. "Work gives evidence of our dignity as
human beings because it reflects the image of God the
Creator in us."[ii] Whether we spend our days checking off
simple mundane tasks or trading on Wall Street, all our work
given to the Lord is holy.[iii] I remember an incident in my
career that powerfully demonstrated to me the reality that
God gives us work – meaningful things to put our hands to.

I found myself scribbling a desperate prayer on a legal tablet
while sitting through yet another long meeting at the college
where I worked. I had enjoyed teaching business for many
years. Although I still liked working with the students, I
found myself at a stalemate. I was not growing and needed
something new to do. So as the meeting went on, my heart
cried out to God for a fresh challenge – something significant
to put my hands to in a new season. I asked Him for
something big that would challenge my leadership skills,
something so demanding I would have to rely upon the Holy
Spirit more than ever for the fulfillment. I was not looking
for a new course to teach or a new task force to lead; I
wanted to do something that had not been done before. This
wasn't necessarily a rational prayer, but it expressed the desire
of my heart.

The Lord loves to engage with us and He heard my prayer.
He heard my prayer! Within a few weeks I was in
conversation with top leaders in my organization, strategizing
ways to implement something radically different from
traditional education. A major challenge was presented which
would dramatically impact our relevance as an institution. We
were at risk of losing a large chunk of community training
business because the largest company in the area was getting
ready to place all their training out for bids in the public
sector. Professionals were tired of the sluggish response of

traditional academia. They were demanding flexible corporate solutions on par with industry standards. This challenge presented a great opportunity and I was invited to lead the charge to create the solution. So, remembering the prayer I had scribbled on that legal tablet and offered up with a sigh, I said "Yes!"

➔**KEY**: Challenge presents divine opportunity.

In that moment I had the vivid realization that, "YES, God made me to do meaningful work." Our God-given work assignment is an invitation worthy of serious consideration. This particular assignment was one I honored, developed, poured over and acted upon with great diligence. I took it to heart; I took it to prayer.

I believe that God loves His children to ask Him for what we need. What thrills my heart even now is the fact that I spoke to the Lord, asking for direction, and He heard me. He used this woman's inquiring heart and spiritual thirst to answer the professional development needs of thousands of people.

I recall praying for wisdom years later when I needed guidance for several business decisions. In response, the Lord gave me a vision of blueprints coming down from heaven with the answers to my prayers. They appeared to be rolled up with labels on the outside designating them for specific needs and problems. This encounter encouraged me to keep praying, finding the answers I needed in conversation with God. My faith was boosted to believe the Lord for direction and to do my part in searching out the blueprints.

In both of these instances I saw incredible results manifest when heavenly equipping and direction met me in the boardroom. Yet so many of us fail to take God up on the invitation to ask how to run a meeting, how to create a proposal, or how to work with a new client. We have not explored the opportunity to work with Him throughout the day as we work in the assignments He has given us.

➔**KEY**: Access blueprints for your work.

About the "Sacred OR Secular" Question

I invite you to come with me on a journey to look further into the heart cry of the one who has a holy calling to teach, to be an entrepreneur, to legislate, to create or to entertain. Together let's dismantle the perceived division between your chosen career path and your personal spiritual significance.

We will examine how this message has become the predominant paradigm for "sacred and secular" callings in western culture. In so doing, we will uncover a surprising position that will free you to do the very thing God has put in your heart to do with diligence and holy abandon.

Threaded throughout this work are real-life stories of individuals who are thriving in their professions in basically every sphere of society while having lasting spiritual impact. We are all designed to participate in ministry as an integral part of our lives and professions.

I believe we have made it too difficult, much harder than it was ever meant to be, to live connected to God in every arena of life. Instead we live divided lives, refusing to embrace what we knew on some level might be true. According to Darrow L. Miller, the biblical worldview provides a framework for viewing every job as something sacred, and for seeing the dignity inherent in all labor.[iv] This concept of work is that it is a vocation – one's calling.[v] It reveals that God is at work in the world, building His kingdom, and that He calls us to participate in the building of His kingdom through our work.

➔**KEY**: Ministry and work go together.

Yes, Paul supported his mission work largely with the labor of his own hands, but if we could go back in time and travel the road with him on his missionary journeys, we would most likely find that in addition to preaching, he also ministered to the people he was making tents, sandals, and belts for *as he worked.*

I believe after considering this book and the humble opinions of both clergy and those in other professions, you will have a base of knowledge that will allow you to settle in your own heart the path that's right for you without sacrificing your innermost desires for significance AND spiritual impact.

There will be peace and no shame in your choice once you reckon with God's gifts, calling and plans for you. The inferiority complex that plagues believers in the marketplace comes from living below our capabilities. Many view as inferior the call of God on their work in the marketplace, and this view transfers to their self image. This book is designed to deliver the information and revelation you need to see yourself and your role rightly. Then you can plug into your place, empowered to supply what others need from you. As you begin to see your work through a new lens you will value your professional contribution to society while feeding your spirit.

To be fully alive in the spiritual, professional and relational arenas of life is to live congruently, allowing these elements to come together so that you are praying, doing great work and caring for people as Jesus did. There is no internal division or conflict; rather there is a wholeness that results when you do not have to use different standards as you move between the different aspects of your life. This type of congruent life is entirely possible.

In a time when scores of self-help books are offered in answer to the aching hearts trying to find a proper place of service, perhaps what is lacking is a spiritual appraisal of God's system and economy which will provide the perspective needed to settle a *life* calling.

In the book of Daniel, the Queen described Daniel as a man "in whom is a spirit of the holy gods…with insight, and wisdom like the gods" (Dan. 5:11). Something was different about Daniel. He performed his work in a foreign king's palace in such a way that he was known as one with "an extraordinary spirit, knowledge and insight, interpretation of dreams, explanation of enigmas, and solver of difficult problems" (Dan. 5:12). How did Daniel earn such a distinguishing reputation serving in a hostile regime?

Daniel established this reputation because he lived a life in partnership with God. We will take an in-depth look at Daniel's track record in a later chapter, but for now suffice it to say that he engaged with the Holy One as he worked.

→**KEY**: Create a distinguishing reputation.

Re-Writing Your Professional Story

If you wonder whether you made a less-than-spiritual choice by working in your professional field…

If you wonder whether you could have a greater impact by going into missions or attending seminary to do the real work…

If you have a secret sense that God is more real to you when you are teaching, working, legislating, banking, making money, or filming and you wonder what's wrong…

Then this message is for you.

But the people who know their God shall be strong, and carry out great exploits. And those of the people who understand shall instruct many (Dan. 11:32b-33a)

The great exploits available for Leader-Believers require a lifestyle of knowing God, not just a quick email devotional you scan and check off your list of duties each day. When we relegate God to an afterthought, we experience a compromised or benched state of existence. Have you ever suffered from a low-grade fever? Are you familiar with that flushed feeling, not really feeling terrible but certainly not feeling very well?

Nothing is more miserable than knowing you are made to run with excellence, having godly impact, but instead finding yourself on the sidelines taking up space. Your energy is drained and you perform sluggishly in whatever you attempt; you lack vitality. A woman who had spent her career operating in this state recently lamented to me, "I wish I had known what I was called to all those years I was still in my job."

It is my hope that you will utilize the tool you hold in your hands to break the low-grade fever pervasive among Leader-Believers in the world today – believers who are not really running the race--not officially quitting, but struggling to simply stay in the game. No one who has ever tasted what it is like to live with fire and abandon wants to live a life of mediocrity. Whether you have tasted it and want it back, or have yet to experience this reality for the first time, you were made for more than mediocrity. Let's get clarity about what our lives are to be as the fragrance of Christ to those around us—a pleasing fragrance of joy and peace—and let's go there together (2 Cor. 2:15). Let's engage with the Holy at work. When we partner with the living God we will do great exploits, bless others and provide lasting value.

Yet who knows whether you have come to the kingdom for such a time as this? (Est. 4:14b)

The world needs you now more than ever as a Leader-Believer to stand confidently at your post as a fully engaged Christian, performing your work in excellence to bless others and please God.

Engage with God

Blueprints for Work

Dear Lord God,

Help Me Engage with the Holy in my Work.

Thank You for the gift of work. Help me to understand Your plans for my professional life and how I may enter into full partnership with You. I embrace You as My God and partner, my Chief Consultant. Give me understanding of how You have placed me in my profession to usher Your presence into the world of my work.

I ask for Your blueprints for my professional life, that I may glorify You. What challenges exist in my work? What divine opportunities lie within these challenges? How can I create a distinguishing reputation by solving problems like Daniel?

Thank You for moving in my professional life. Open my eyes to see the opportunities You place before me. Show me practical ways I can serve others at work. Teach me how to know You better, how to hear Your voice, and how to follow You in bringing Your presence into my work.

Jesus, help me re-write my professional story that I may engage in greater measure with the Holy at work.

I believe You have brought me here for such a time as this.

In Jesus Name,

Signed:

Date:

Chapter 2
The What: Bringing God's Presence in the Workplace – Your Sacred Calling

"Not by might nor by power, but by My Spirit," says the Lord of hosts. (Zech. 4:6b)

To break us out of our low-grade fever, we must identify the culprit – our infected thinking which tells us our work doesn't count on a spiritual level. The false argument that our work and the sacred are two different things must be confronted with the truth. "We speak of those in 'full-time ministry' as if only they are 'full-time Christians.'"[vi]

What Does God Think About Work?

Genesis opens with God at work creating the earth. Have you ever thought about the fact that He wasn't preaching or conducting a crusade? He was building, designing, gardening; He was working. Then He gave work to man (Gen. 1:26-28). Adam and Eve were responsible for ruling over and tending the earth in relationship with God. We read of God enjoying dialog with them as they tended the garden. They didn't have to wait till they got off work to meet with Him.

When Jesus healed a man on the Sabbath, he incurred the wrath of the Pharisees for causing a man to "work" by getting up and carrying his pallet on the day of rest. This would seem a minor point since the man was healed after thirty-eight years of sickness. I love Jesus' answer to His critics: "My Father is working until now and I Myself am working" (John 5:17). Jesus received His inspiration for work from His Father. This is the perfect picture of our work being inspired by God.

Based on these scriptural examples, we can safely conclude that work is from God. In fact, He involved man in work right away. Paul strongly acknowledges the value of work in Colossians 3:23, "Whatever you do, work at it with all your heart, as working for the Lord and not for men…" When we acknowledge that the Lord has given us our work and we offer it back to Him, it is holy, it is sacred. In fact, on the day Christ Himself asks us about our lives, we will give an answer to questions such as these: Were you faithful? Did you work hard? Are you someone who just worked to please other people or did you work with genuine righteousness?[vii]

The healing recognition that our work, is sacred,[viii] inspired by God and performed for Him, is the springboard that will launch us into the understanding of how to bring the presence of God into our spheres of influence. As we accept God's invitation to embrace our work as sacred, we can expand the concept of our individual work to the collective mandate of Leader-Believers. When individuals work together bringing God's presence into an organization or city, the results are compounded and we begin to see how God's presence impacts a region. It is exciting to realize we are part of God's work on a larger scale and gives us greater vision for our individual part of the story.

So yes, your work is a large expression of your calling and your calling is sacred. Not only is it "okay" to view yourself as engaging with the Holy in your work, it is the *only* way to perform your work as a Leader-Believer.

Some Helpful Definitions

Many people are searching for clarity regarding their workplace calling in this hour. You are not the only one looking for books like the one you now hold. As you search for truth, you will find more than one answer. There are many approaches, views and even ministries that address the ache in the working man's heart for sacred validation. I want to briefly examine two of the primary answers being offered to people in your position. My purpose is not to provide an exhaustive discourse on all of the labels or terms applied to work as sacred, (i.e. "transformational business," "kingdom business," etc.), but to give you a grid for interpreting the many answers offered to marketplace believers.

Those with a passion to utilize business as a vehicle to carry the gospel, both financially and physically, to other locations will identify with the philosophy of Business As Mission (BAM). The term BAM was defined by the Lausanne Committee for World Evangelization in 2004 as follows: "Business in and of itself is the ministry and instrument of mission. It is about releasing the entrepreneurs and business professionals within the church in order to transform the world through their business activities." Business relationships provide a context for living and sharing the gospel in the normal course of a day's work. Organizations such as Youth with a Mission (YWAM) and Business Professional Network (BPN) provide opportunities for western world businesses to operate missionally as they take their work abroad. BAM is intentional about taking the gospel "to all peoples," seeking out places of greatest spiritual and financial need.[ix]

A larger sector of our population will resonate with the philosophy of Workplace Ministries. The Workplace Ministry approach addresses Leader-Believers who are "taking the gospel to people where they work, with integration of Biblical principles into every aspect of business practice."[x] This philosophy applies to men and women working in any setting. Workplace prayer groups and Bible studies are examples of Workplace Ministry, as well as working with character and integrity.

What Do These Answers Mean for You?

If you are a business owner, you are probably already thinking about how you might involve your company or organization in BAM or your employees in Workplace Ministry. Some of you are thinking about the owners and leaders of your company – and you already have a good idea whether or not they would be open to these philosophies. However, many of you are probably feeling hemmed in because you are in a company or organization that would never welcome any overt expression of your values and faith. You may feel these options are out of your reach.

Before you get too far in your analysis, let's pause for a moment of truth. The answer to this question does not lie with your company owner, leader, the HR Department, or even your boss.

(You may be thinking, "But you don't know my boss?!")

The issue is not your job description or the philosophy of your organization. Your hunger to be released in fullness and used by God to impact your world for the better will genuinely be fed when you acknowledge and satisfy the hunger for God in your own spirit. The answer is within you. You are meant to bring God's presence regardless of where you work and what kind of environment you are in.

Open your mouth wide and I will fill it.
(Psa. 81:10b, NAS)

Your internal response to God will bring His presence in your place of assignment. Each individual Leader-Believer can impact their sphere of influence by engaging with the Holy One. To engage the Holy One is to connect with Him relationally. When we reckon with this central issue, the Holy Spirit recalibrates all the other questions.

> ➔**KEY**: The internal reality of engaging with the Holy transcends your external circumstances.

The workplace ministry philosophies described earlier are designed to facilitate the entrance of the Holy Spirit in your place of employment – but they are not the Spirit Himself. At the end of the day, we cannot rely on a program to release something we do not carry ourselves. This begs the question, how will we bring God's presence forth to impact our spheres of influence?

Once we offer our work unto the Lord, we desire to remain engaged *as we go* through our day. The Lord does not send us to work, He goes with us to work and thus the Holy Spirit counsels and directs us as we learn to respond to Him in the midst of our routine. At times we may take a moment to pray, while at other times we may find ourselves praying without ceasing through the awareness that He is with us even when we are fully available to our work and those around us.

> ➔**KEY**: We cannot bring a presence we do not carry.

Regardless of the path we take in our search for the sacred at work, if we do not engage the Holy One then we have just selected another program to sign up for and prolonged our low-grade fever. We must break through to a healing place. A fever serves a critical purpose, notifying us that that the body

19

is fighting off an attack. When we take the medicine required to eradicate the sickness, the fever is alleviated and we get back to healthy, vibrant living. In the same way, we can be thankful for the misery and lack of fulfillment that has brought us to the Great Physician who can heal not only the body but also the spirit of a man or woman yearning to embrace their calling.

Just as the burned-out missionary runs the risk of allowing their work to become the focus rather than the Lord, the Leader-Believer can fall prey to the same sickness and promote a business as their mission or a workplace as their ministry while neglecting the main thing: engaging with the Holy in their work.

How many times do we find ourselves far from engaging with the Holy in the crush of life, work, politics, conflicts, relationships and the demands of living? How do we protect so precious a calling?

Look for His Presence

"As we do our work while praying on some level, the line between action and adoration disappears."[xi] At that point we are agile, flexible, committed to the Holy One Himself, and alive in our callings – and it is our goal to remain in that sweet spot, communing with Him.

A Man after God's Own Heart

So you ask, "By the way, has this actually been done before?" Good question. If anyone had a busy job, it was David with a kingdom to run, battles to fight and affairs of the nation of Israel to govern. He had to deal with internal turmoil, bloodthirsty generals and rebellious children. Even so, David went after the most important thing: bringing the presence of God to his city.

David learned to be faithful doing the everyday work of a shepherd on the hillside. Later in life he took on military and political roles, but his time as a shepherd prepared him to lead his people in both roles. (Psa. 78:70-72). As a shepherd boy he wrote many of the psalms and sang them to God. Communicating with God, meditating on the Law and even writing songs about it instilled in his heart the truths that would sustain him throughout his life. The time alone with God as a young man shaped his thoughts and view of God. He desired to be with God above all else. Although not perfectly, we see that David engaged with the Holy. God called him a man after His own heart (Acts 13:22). David understood what God wanted from him and he developed a passionate partnership with God, accomplishing the will of God despite his failures.

→**KEY**: Keep your faith when no one sees; become trained for tests others *will* see.

David became a significant king after enduring difficult tests which further refined his character. His years of waiting on the Lord as a shepherd and a fugitive transformed his way of working and equipped him to take on the challenges of governing Israel in a period of great political and military turmoil. David won many political and relational battles by inquiring of the Lord to learn what he should do in each instance (2 Sam. 5:19).

→**KEY**: Inquire of the Lord.

Interestingly, after his succession to the throne David omitted one very important prerequisite for successful impact. He went after the Ark of the Covenant (which carried the presence of God) without seeking the presence of God on the matter.

In his procession to acquire the Ark, David took with him 30,000 choice men of Israel. I imagine his track record of success due to God's favor left him either somewhat giddy or overly confident. In the great procession, Uzzah defied protocol when he reached out to steady the ark with his hand and was struck dead immediately.

➔ **KEY**: Don't disqualify yourself based on past failures.

How devastating to David, who had such high hopes and plans to bring the very presence of God into the midst of the city...only to experience tragic results. I have no doubt David was angry and afraid and questioned how he could ever bring the Ark of the Covenant to Jerusalem.

➔ **KEY**: A Leader-Believer does what it takes to learn from mistakes.

Finally David realized he had not inquired of the Lord for strategy and protocol (1 Chron. 15:13). Even though he was going after God's presence contained in the Ark, he neglected His own partnership with the Lord by rushing to conclusions without the necessary dialog. He attempted to take a shortcut.

A Right Way to Bring the Presence

David returned to transport the Ark in the proper way. The zeal and abandon demonstrated by David's actions in bringing the Ark paint a picture of our mandate to bring the very presence of God into our own jobs, work, and cities. We too in our haste to "do God's work" can fail to seek Him in the prescribed way, and we can also incur negative results. We all know the coworker who goes by the name of Christian but alienates most people around them with brash tactics.

Just as David partnered passionately with God, stood the tests of his destiny, and learned to inquire of God to bring the presence, modern day men and women in the workplace must also engage in relationship with God and seek His presence. Engaging with the Holy implies relationship. From this relationship with the Lord, men and women derive the pleasure of His presence.

→ **KEY**: God doesn't desire robots, He desires friends.

Untapped Powerhouse for Working in the Presence

Even when we embrace our callings and desire to bring God's presence in all we do, we are faced with a real-world marketplace that is quite brutal, competitive and uncertain. Today's Leader-Believer is faced with the pressure to make wise decisions and form creative solutions. In light of your overloaded schedule, jam packed with meetings and deadlines, you don't have space for "engaging with the Holy" on your To-Do List. And you are right; what we are talking about is not just one more thing to do, it is a completely new operating system.

A requirement for day-to-day business in any arena is the ability to run with excellence in the pressure-cooker of life. Such a highly charged environment requires a depth of spiritual guidance beyond what we have accessed in the past. I would propose to you that there is a spiritual reservoir of God's presence, a new operating system, available to today's Leader-Believer in the workplace; it is found in the Holy Spirit. We don't have the luxury of doing "business as usual." When you seek His presence first and foremost, the Lord will release blessing, grace and solutions in your work.

→ **KEY**: Upgrade to the Holy Spirit Operating System.

How much more will your heavenly Father give the Holy Spirit to those who ask Him. (Luke 11:13b)

God's presence was so important to Moses that we see him refusing to go on with his assignment unless that presence went with him (Exod. 33:12-15). God's presence is described as rest, joy, and gladness (Acts 2:28; Psa. 16:11). Elsewhere, we find verses describing the effects of God's presence as grace, glory, goodness and compassion (Exod. 33:15-23).

How long has it been since we waited on God's presence to plan our workweek with rest, joy, and gladness? Even though we have the Holy Spirit, we must still learn to rest, quiet ourselves and wait on God's peace and presence in the midst of our busy lives. What workplace couldn't be transformed by demonstrating simple goodness and genuine compassion as we work together and serve our customers?

So how can we describe the Holy Spirit? In Isaiah 11:2 we find this description:

1. Spirit of the Lord
2. Spirit of wisdom
3. Spirit of understanding
4. Spirit of counsel
5. Spirit of might
6. Spirit of knowledge
7. Fear of the Lord

What could we possibly need that is not available in the Holy Spirit? When I review a resume, I take a look at the skills and competencies a person brings to the table. The Holy Spirit brings to the table not only a complete set of credentials, but the reality of who God is – His very presence. When we need to know what to do, how to plan, where to go, how to navigate, or how to bring the presence of the Lord, we have everything we need in Him.

Blueprints for Your Sphere of Influence

As Leader-Believers we have the distinct privilege, dare I say responsibility, to ask for and access spiritual guidance from the throne room of heaven for our decisions and strategies. Many of us are accustomed to seeking the Lord for family and church decisions, but what about our professional strategies and blueprints for work? What would it look like to access heaven's wisdom for your business, your governmental role, your classroom, media project or customer service job?

My enthusiasm for relying on heavenly resources is fueled by my experience in developing a corporate training center guided by the Spirit. My prayers for a new career challenge found heaven's ear as I scribbled my desires on that yellow tablet during a long meeting. I should have been paying attention to the speaker's address, but my heart took me elsewhere as I longed for a new challenge. Just days later, I was called to a meeting with community leaders who expressed concern over the lack of corporate training available to the key industries responsible for our local economy.

Over the next twelve years I had the privilege of starting and leading a highly successful corporate learning center reaching over 150,000 participants. The challenges of rapid growth, demanding projects, the need for specialized talent, and the development of systems and client relationships landed me and my fledgling staff in an incubator to watch God's guidance at work. I knew no other way to approach these challenges than through processing, prayer, lots of coffee and implementing heaven's plans. Learning to flow in the Holy Spirit operating system became a way of doing business that resulted in a high performance team of employees, satisfied clients and profitable business. Visitors from around the globe came to see this good work.

Action Plan to Access the Blueprints

For the eyes of the Lord move to and fro throughout the earth that He may strongly support those whose heart is completely His. (2 Chron. 16:9a, NASB)

We are looking for the Lord to support us in today's challenging workplace environment. He is looking to help those who seek Him above all else, fully investing in divine relationship. In this relationship, as we search for each other, we are right on track to engage with the Holy.

Could it be that the Holy Spirit, seated in the throne room yet searching the earth for a devoted heart, casts a jealous side glance at today's Leader-Believer who bypasses the powerhouse of the Spirit of God for the world's wisdom? The leader I speak of is not willing to go to the place of devotion in the inner chambers of prayer to approach the Holy Spirit.

Let us not give the Spirit reason for jealousy. Begin to ask God to reveal where you are accessing worldly wisdom. Self help books and secular wisdom abound, but they all pale in comparison to the wisdom from the throne room of heaven. I would even encourage you to make a list of areas in your business or work where you need heaven's counsel. Then actively engage with the Holy Spirit to hear from heaven and develop your action plan. Search the Word, pray, and give attention to God's ways.

Experience the Sacred Life (don't just read about it)

This sacred calling within you is the reason you hold this book in your hands. Because the Lord wants you to know your calling (it is He who is calling you) and desires that you live it out in partnership with Him, it is worth your time to engage with the Holy in the experience provoked by encountering the truth in this book. Notice I am asking you to experience, not merely read, this book.

If you will take time now to look at how you can carry the presence of God at work, you will position yourself for exponential growth in the realms of impact and influence. First, though, you have a few decisions to make in the course of this reading. As you interact with the text and allow the Holy Spirit to guide you, you have the opportunity to embrace the sacred in your work. This opportunity will be lost, however, unless you drive a stake in the ground so you will be able to run with your plan in the future. I promise you will need to return to this place when you find yourself disconnecting from what you know to be true about your calling due to the busyness of life and the well meaning but misinformed voices labeling work as secular. So heads up: get out your iPad, your notepad, your recorder, even write in this book and about this book. Blog your journey, tell your closest associates what you are doing and invite them to join you. Write the vision plainly now so you can run with it for the long haul (Hab. 2:2).

A Marketplace Awakening

The resurgence of the message of the holy calling of the worker in the workplace, the marketplace, is God's way of answering the critical question on the mind of the working body of Christ in our day. An army of men and women in all spheres of society are being awakened to their holy calling and learning how to stand in their places, bringing God's presence. There is need of and room for every man and woman to step into their sacred calling in this hour.

The days grow dark with legislation opposed to the family, fraudulent business practices, a media which promotes death and immorality, an education system which encroaches on godly values, and the demise of a once Christian culture.

However, our light shines brighter in the darkness and this is your time to shine brightly, bringing the presence of God as only you can.

> *Light arises in the darkness for the upright;*
> *(Psa. 112:4a, NAS)*

As individuals respond to the call of God in the marketplace, we will see that we are on God's timeline at a unique moment in history. I dare say we are on the precipice of a great awakening in the marketplace. Leader-Believers are no longer content to sit idly by when they are called to shine in greatness.

> *Arise, shine; For your light has come! And the glory of*
> *the LORD is risen upon you. (Isaiah 60:1)*

This is your time to arise and shine.

Engage with the Holy

Bringing the Presence

Oh Lord,

Thank you Lord that I am carrying Your presence with me as I pursue the callings and tasks You have given me today. I want to arise, to go about the day full of Your Spirit.

Lord show me Your blueprints today as we do the work.

Bring me closer into Your thoughts and plans as we engage today. I give you my plans my work my assignments and am experiencing great hope and anticipation that You are with me, helping me, showing me how to walk this out.

Lord help my coworkers, others in my company or store or school or organization to be encouraged when they interact with me because I am showing goodness and compassion to consider them like You do. Thank you for the opportunities coming my way to bring the presence of God by the way I interact with coworkers, my boss, my customers or students or the public in any way. May I change the atmosphere for the better because we are teamed up divinely, You and me Lord.

In Jesus Name,

Signed:

Date:

Chapter 3
The Why: You Were Made for Impact

*...that you may know what is the hope of His calling
(Eph. 1:18a)*

Now that we have acknowledged the fact that we are all born
to engage with the Holy in our work, bringing God's
presence, we need to explore the impact our lives and work
are meant to have on those around us. The realization that we
were made for impact is a game changer and requires that we
take the time to understand God's mandate for greatness in
our lives. In our exploration of the mandate, we will identify
the desires behind our search for impact and discover how to
find ultimate fulfillment in knowing God. We will look at
church history to see why we bought the lie that our
professional lives are disconnected and separate from our
spiritual lives in the first place. Empowered with this arsenal
of understanding, we will bring the Holy into the workplace
again in meaningful partnership with God.

Our Search for Impact: We Desire Greatness

Pursuing a career in any field is a pointless goal if not tied to a
meaningful outcome beyond attaining a job title and reaching

a certain income level. The journey of professional growth is filled with ups and downs, victories and challenges, all leading to a lifetime of lessons learned – but this is not enough. Even if the trip to success is challenging and exhilarating, at some point questions such as these must be answered: *What was this for? What is the point? What is all this unto? For what greater purpose did I do the work, labor the long hours, sweat the small stuff and tackle the big stuff?*

Immediate rewards of financial gain, recognition or satisfaction may distract us from answering the ultimate question: "What was the significance of my work?" Eventually, we must consider this question. If we find ourselves at the culmination of a career or any season of life without ever having anchored our efforts in lasting meaning, the opportunity for impact will be gone and the end-result found lacking. For this reason I want to urge you to answer the question sooner rather than later.

The search for significance is a universal cry of the human heart. Mike Bickle explores this reality in his book *The Seven Longings of the Human Heart*, where he describes the areas in which we find ourselves reaching for more:

> The Longing to Be Enjoyed by God
> The Longing for Fascination
> The Longing for Beauty
> The Longing for Greatness
> The Longing for Intimacy without Shame
> The Longing to Be Wholehearted
> The Longing to Make a Deep and Lasting Impact[xii]

Every man and woman yearns for validation in their desire to be great, to be not only loved but enjoyed by God, and to live wholeheartedly, leaving a lasting mark on those around them. Few of us realize these innate desires are designed to draw us toward knowing God better. When we look to Him for our fulfillment, we have employed our desires to their greatest end – to God's glory and for our good.

God is the Ultimate Fulfillment of Desire

Not only do we desire to have these longings fulfilled, but God longs to become our ultimate fulfillment. Such knowledge is a refreshing contrast to the pop psychology books which can lead us into a wrongly placed focus on self. Pride and self-promotion are sure deterrents to a meaningful life of impact. When we lack the vital knowledge that God's leadership over our lives is perfect, we often attempt to take on the job that only God can do and seek to fulfill our desires on our own, outside of Him.

> *For promotion cometh neither from the east, nor from the west, nor from the south. But God is the judge; he putteth down one, and setteth up another. (Psa. 75:6-7, KJV)*

The quest for greater impact absolutely can be fulfilled in your life whether you are an entrepreneur or a full-time pastor when you embark on the journey to find your fulfillment in God's great love.

God's Participation in Our Journey

> *The Lord looks from heaven;*
> *He sees all the sons of men.*
> *From the place of His dwelling He looks*
> *On all the inhabitants of the earth;*
> *He fashions their hearts individually;*
> *He considers all their works. (Psa. 33:13-15)*

God pays close attention to every level of His creation. Consider all the realms ranging from the heavens down to the sons of men, and see how intricately God is involved in each of them. Notice how mindful the Lord is of His creation as indicated by the actions listed in this passage: He is "looking, seeing, fashioning, and considering" what is going on in the realms of heaven and earth. God's interest in our lives is far from passive—it's thoughtful, intentional, and considerate of all the realms or strata of His creation. He sees our work, hears our prayers, and understands our hearts.

When I marvel at a glorious sunset and ponder the reality that the God who created the earth is also concerned with my life and business plan, it instantly calibrates my sense of worth and belonging. I am amazed that whether I have a day of simple tasks ahead or I am launching a strategic initiative, the Lord is considering my work.

Do you ever find yourself acting one way when you are alone and another when you know someone *important* is watching? Don't answer that out loud, but I know the answer because I have done the same thing! We must realize that God is right alongside us, watching our work each and every day.

God desires to be our primary partner. He takes pleasure in our company, our prayers and our reach for Him. He delights in watching us work out our destiny in Him. The dialog, the relationship and the unfolding mystery we find emerging when we actively partner with God in our assignments (whether we are running a family household, a taco stand, a large company, or an entire country) – this is the heart of the matter. He invites us to know Him. Knowing God beckons you into the partnership of your life.

➔**KEY**: You are invited to partner with God.

Before God spoke the world into creation, He desired fellowship with man. Although God is sovereign, He is not a disinterested leader who simply issues commands and refuses discussion. Instead He remains actively interested and involved in how things are playing out and welcomes us into the dialog on several levels. He wants us to partner with Him through prayer and action in the governing of our individual lives, our cities, and our nations. Let's look at biblical evidence of God's desire for partnership with individual men and women.

Why did Jesus turn water into wine at the wedding in Cana when He had just said it wasn't time yet? Was it in response to Mary's words? It was evident by her comments that she expected Jesus to solve the problem, and He did (John 2:1-5).

Why did Jesus deliver the daughter of the Syro-Phoenician woman after He told her, in essence, to be on her way and "not to steal the children's bread?" Was it because the woman "kept asking?" She stayed in the dialog with Jesus, reminding Him that even the dogs have crumbs to eat.

> *And He said to her, "Because of this answer go; the demon has gone out of your daughter." And going back to her home, she found the child lying on the bed, the demon having left. (Mark 7:29-30)*

God watched to see if Moses would turn aside to explore the burning bush; when he did, God called his name (Exod. 3:4). What might have happened if Moses hadn't turned aside? God was about to issue a call on Moses' life to lead His people out of captivity. We see God's intense interest in Moses' reaction to the burning bush in this encounter.

Before He destroyed Sodom and Gomorrah for their depravity, the Lord informed Abraham of His plan because of their relationship. The Lord said, "Shall I hide from Abraham what I am doing?" (Gen. 18:17). "I have known him," the Lord said, speaking again of their relationship. So the Lord made a decision to inform Abraham of his plan. Abraham countered respectfully by asking the Lord to spare the city if there were fifty righteous people discovered in it.

The Lord agreed. Abraham countered, what if there were only forty-five? The Lord agreed. Or forty? The Lord agreed. Or thirty? The Lord agreed. Or twenty? The Lord agreed. Or ten? The Lord agreed (Gen. 18:17-33).

These accounts reflect a God who dialogs and partners with men and women in the affairs of life and business. These are but a few examples of those who not only engaged with God but dared to stay in the discussion to taste the best wine at a wedding, see a child set free from the devil, see a leader step into a national deliverance calling, or deliberate the fate of a city.

→**KEY**: God is not looking for silent partners.

RSVP: God's Invitation Demands a Response

To understand the end-goal that *all we do should lead us and others closer to knowing the Lord and knowing Him better* gives enhanced meaning to all the pieces of the big plan. Our individual journeys are taking us closer to the day when everyone on the earth will stand in awe of our great God (Psa. 33:8).

How can we play a greater part in advancing this great day when all mankind will recognize the glory of the Lord? We can trust Him to create the perfect development plan for our lives that will result in knowing Him better and running in our unique lanes, our true power alleys, to bring lasting impact.

→**KEY**: Run in your power alley.

The term "power alley" describes the combination of spiritual and natural gifts, talents and knowledge a Leader-Believer accesses while working in partnership with God.

When a Leader-Believer works in partnership with God, he or she finds freedom in their power alley to work from a foundation of getting to know God. Such an invitation beckons us to operate in relationship with God with freedom to bring our unique personality to our assignment. Working in our power alley does not equate to feeling "qualified" for the assignment. It is not as much about our qualifications as it is Who we are partnering with and our follow-through.

How will you respond to the invitation to know your God, to work with Him, to interact with Him strategically, to fulfill your destiny in Him? Will you lay it aside with the rest of the mail and get to it later or will you choose to embrace the call to know Him and run headlong into His arms, settling your quandary? Are you willing to have your life completely changed and calibrated to the heart of God? I realize these are heavy questions and I challenge you to wrestle them through because to set this invitation aside for consideration at a later date will cost you the vitality of your spiritual walk now.

➔ **KEY:** The golden key is to partner with God.

For this discussion, our partnership with God concerns how to go about fulfilling our destiny and calling to further God's glory. In a business partnership it is expected that investments are made and returns are realized. The partners will discuss the goals of the business, the assignments of each partner, and come to an agreement on how to conduct the business. God has made the ultimate investment with the gift of His Son Jesus Christ who died for our salvation and rose again. He also invests in our lives through the resources He has given us. Resources can include natural talents, spiritual gifts, education and training, land or money, relationships, or opportunities.

We respond by investing time and energy to pursue the assignment and call on our lives. As we go about the business of life, like any good partner we want to continue dialoging and getting feedback and direction from our partner. The reality of partnering with God through listening and responding is not unlike that of communicating with a business partner, except that our partnership with the Lord is fueled by love. He first loved us. His love quickens our hearts to respond. Because He loved us we love Him back. The response of love grows our relationship with God as we pursue Him, finding our life destiny in Him. God is not a silent partner or a secret investor. He has disclosed Himself as the one who loves us, inciting our response of love for Him (John 14:21).

The Great Disconnect

If in fact God is working out a plan that extends beyond our salvation to living meaningful lives by partnering with Him, then where did the disconnect in our society between work and spirituality come from? In my wrestling with this question I have discovered the heart of the matter is actually a disconnect from the full message of the gospel. I was saddened to realize that so many believers have been presented a partial gospel and am relieved to share the whole story. By taking a look at church history we can identify where this latter part of the gospel message took a back seat to salvation and eventually disappeared for all practical purposes in Christian discipleship. The full gospel story told in the Bible includes what some call Four Chapters:

1. Creation
2. Fall
3. Redemption
4. Restoration[xiii]

In the past two centuries, churches in the western world have limited the presentation of the gospel to two chapters: the fall (our sinful condition) and redemption (our salvation). In other words, it is all about *our* sin and *our* salvation, leaving us with an anemic gospel and we have even perpetuated this incomplete version of the gospel among those we evangelize. These two glorious realities are taken from the middle of the story of God and man; the loss of the first and last chapters is where the expectation of meaningful work in our professional lives died. If we are convicted of sin and are saved, then Hallelujah, we have the *whole* gospel! Or do we? We are left to fill our time with work that doesn't necessarily "count" and serves no greater purpose other than putting food on the table and supplying tithes and offerings.

When you get ready to read a new book, what is the first thing you look at? The back cover, right? Some even read the last chapter just to know how the story ends. Without understanding that our lives are meant to play a part in the restoration story, we have made decisions about how to live void of the final chapter. I liken this to reading a novel, thinking you know how it will end, and putting the book down too early when the final chapter was far grander than your assumptions and imagination could anticipate. The story of the gospel ends with the restoration of all things, and we have robbed ourselves of the glorious vision of our role in that restoration by accepting a partial gospel story.[xiv]

The two-chapter gospel accentuates our wounds. The four-chapter gospel elevates our worth as image-bearers of God.[xv] Yes we have fallen, yes we are saved, and yes we participate in the restoration work of the gospel through our work. God has a great development plan for your life as a result of your salvation. He invites you to partner in the full story of the gospel. You are right to enter into it with all your heart.

Foundations of the Partnership: Articles of Incorporation

We will talk about how to practically fulfill our assignment in partnership with God in a later chapter, but let's recognize and establish our foundational assignment in the partnership now. Every Leader-Believer is called to these two mandates:

1. The Mandate of Love – Loving Well
2. The Great Commission – Teaching and Training

As we become more like Him, we value what He values. These mandates to live the fulfilled Christian life apply no matter what our jobs may be. We are all in danger of becoming so familiar with these mandates and associated passages, that we lose sight of their power and truth. Let's examine them together.

The Mandate of Love

Jesus called the commandment to love the Lord our God with all our heart and mind and soul the greatest commandment (Matt. 22:37-38). The second commandment is to love our neighbor as we love ourselves (Matt. 22:39). In fact if we do our work without love we are simply adding to the noise factor (1 Cor. 13:1). The love we have received from God enables us to love those around us, even the unlovely (1 John 4:19). Jesus said in John 17:26,

> ...and I have made Your name known to them, and will make it known, so that the love with which You loved Me may be in them, and I in them.

I confess that I have read these scriptures about love many times and yet I desperately needed a revelation of His love. We have used the word love trivially for so long that I lost touch with its deeper meaning. What is Jesus speaking of when He says that God will love us just like God loves Jesus? What does that kind of love look like?

Let me invite you to read my personal account of God's great love for one person, my brother. I have chosen this account because it is a story where God showed such great love that I hope I never get past it.

I lost my brother suddenly in 2012 within four weeks of a diagnosis of a terminal lung disease. He had dropped to less than a hundred pounds as the pulmonary fibrosis robbed his energy and greatly diminished his body over the course of a year. Up till then we had not known what disease ravaged his body. When the diagnosis did come, he finally had a label for the problem, but there was no solution. The disease was in the advanced stages; the doctors told us we had six months to two years. "You aren't supposed to have to bury your little brother," I remember musing during the fast-paced drama that unfolded over an intense month, the last month of his life. And yet, I did.

Experiencing the pain of sudden loss and the exhilaration of watching God set things in order to remove all offense marked me with an overwhelming sense of awe at His desire to touch one heart. God surrounded my brother with so much love in the last four weeks he had on this earth, after he had experienced the pain of loneliness for many years. We all felt God's nearness. I was reminded of how Jesus wept with Mary and Martha, feeling their agony, embracing their pain. We began to observe many acts of mercy that were undeniably from God's hand, such as my brother being called to the front of the line in the ER waiting room where hundreds of patients had been waiting for hours. His eyes grew wide as we wheeled him back and he looked at me like, "Can you believe they called us up first?" Later I heard my brother speaking to a friend on the phone of how God had moved him to the front of the line.

God was moving my brother to the front of the line in many ways. I watched the Lord take away every offense, clear every hard question, and wrap my brother in love as I drove him on the long car ride from his home to mine to live with us for what we expected to be at least six months. Over the two-day drive, I was keenly aware that God was ministering to my brother and showing him heaven. I wondered if it could possibly be that the time was shorter than we expected. Dan opened his heart wide that day as he exclaimed to me like a boy in wonder, "Lin, you know the verse in Psalms that says God is our refuge?! I LOVE that verse!"

The Lord took my brother during a glorious sunset on the second day of our trip, and the timing was God's kiss to me because the sunset is my love language with God. If the sun is setting and it is possible, I will be out on a porch or peering out a window to watch and to commune with my God.

I saw through tears with eyes wide open how Jesus loved my brother to the end! Now he waits with others in the cloud of witnesses for me. This time *he* has gone ahead.

Do we know what love is? We must find out. How can we know this love? Do we begin to understand what God has done for us? Do we have any idea how He intervenes on our behalf? Oh friend of God, we must find out if we are to have any lasting impact. For you see, no matter what we accomplish in our mandate, if it is without a revelation of love we waste our lives.

How will you fulfill your mandate in love? Are you willing to be the answer to your own prayer on behalf of a worker or family member? I had prayed for the Lord to set my brother in a family (Psa. 68:6). He chose to set him in our family for a short time. I was the answer God had in mind to my own request, and it was the honor of my life.

In my workplace, I have also learned to love. Many favorite stories of this love for teams and employees in my sphere of influence are found in *Find your Why Forward*.[xvi] You have the invitation to create your own stories of kindness expressed through your work relationships.

Teaching and Training: The Great Commission

Such love compels us to action. The Great Commission describes distinct actions we will take for the sake of love. These actions revolve around inviting others into the exhilarating mandate for impact. Let's look at the scripture designated as the Great Commission:

> *Go therefore and make disciples of all the nations, baptizing them in the name of the Father and of the Son and of the Holy Spirit, teaching them to observe all things that I have commanded you; and lo, I am with you always, even to the end of the age. Amen (Matt. 28:19-20)*

This scripture is most often used to teach Christians to bring others to Christ through salvation and baptism. This is essential; but what about the "teaching?" Who are we teaching? The nations? And what about the last proclamation of God's love that brings the Great Commission to its conclusion, underlining that we are together with God while we perform these actions? Let's take a look at this familiar verse in The Message:

> *Jesus, undeterred, went right ahead and gave his charge: "God authorized and commanded me to commission you: Go out and train everyone you meet, far and near, in this way of life, marking them by baptism in the threefold name: Father, Son, and Holy Spirit. Then instruct them in the practice of all I have commanded you. I'll be with you as you do this, day after day after day, right up to the end of the age. (MSG)*

We will teach and train others of the One we know and love by the very way we work and live our lives. Teaching requires that we know something about the ones we are teaching, understand their needs and questions, and invite them into their own divine partnership with God.

To be a teacher or a trainer implies that we have something to offer, something of value, something of worth to teach. We have studied the Christian life of partnership, experienced it, and are still growing in partnership as we teach.

> → **KEY**: The life lessons of a Leader-Believer
> are often the very thing that will move another person
> forward in life.

To learn from another's success, to avoid repeating their pain, to leverage their life experiences – this is hard to put a price tag on. Many are craving a teacher or mentor. We have what others need: we have love, we are walking in partnership with God, and we have the practical instruction to now teach this to others around us.

Some believers will physically travel to another nation to teach spreading the gospel. Many others will teach in banks, schools, shops, city halls and recording studios as they partner with God, fulfilling their assignments. Teaching plays out differently according to your role in your particular sphere of influence. For instance, I taught young leaders on my staff and others I was mentoring by virtue of being a leader in the corporate world. In ministry, my husband and I mentored young couples to assume roles of leadership in the church and take our places. Others are teachers by occupation, but we are all forever teaching formally or informally as we carry out the Great Commission.

Jesus completed His commission with the statement, "Lo, I am *with you* always, even to the end of the age." The emphasis on relationship, partnership and nearness to us is expressed clearly in this passage so often used to instruct us in the Christian life. Do we realize we were never meant to live that life alone? Even in this mandate for reaching the world with the gospel, our Lord chose to emphasize the fact that He is with us.

→**KEY**: Isolation is a great enemy of the Christian life, yet we are never alone.

We need His constant companionship and we need to enter into fellowship with other believers. In Acts 2:42 we read that the believers continually devoted themselves to teaching, fellowship, breaking of bread and to prayer. Intentional involvement in the lives of other believers points again to the value of relationships that will enable us to carry out our mandate of the Great Commission. Loving our co-workers enough to train them along the way, day by day, transaction by transaction, meeting by meeting, as we model our partnership with God will cause them to desire their own partnership with Him.

We see in Daniel 11:32 it is the people that *know their God* who do great exploits. Then by all means, let us pursue knowing our God. In this vein we will do the great exploits while sustaining our vital relationship with God. Otherwise we risk losing our relationship in pursuit of the activity of the partnership.

How do we apply the Articles of Incorporation?

Here is what it looks like for me. As an individual who works in the marketplace to develop leaders, I rely on God, my Chief Consultant, to give me tips on how to best meet the needs of my clients. Whether my clients are believers in Jesus or not, I pray for them. The Lord will highlight areas of need in their lives and show me how to develop their leadership skills.

Some clients will never know I have prayed for them. With others, because of the way the relationship develops, I will have clear invitations to let them know. I never impose my agenda on my clients. I am there to serve them. The amazing thing is watching how God orchestrates events, divine appointments and training sessions so that I am bringing His presence. Often this happens without ever opening a Bible or praying out loud on the platform and giving an altar call. Truth is truth no matter where you are and God doesn't need a PR agent to announce His credentials. He simply needs active partners who work with Him.

One of my professional clients began working with me to navigate politics in an organization where she had been quickly promoted. We addressed nonverbal communication, managing change, and how to take the reins of her new authority in a way that built bridges with the existing leaders. After six months of executive coaching, I noticed a drastic change in the way she was handling conflict. It had lost its power over her because she had become secure in the Lord.

How did we integrate the spiritual conversations in our consulting meetings? I simply asked the questions and it came out of her mouth. She began to hear herself telling her own story of spiritual disappointment. She also heard herself describe beginning to partner with her God, getting to know Him and working with Him. The new confidence in her voice and the composure with which she is navigating a white water rapid of transition is due to her response in her partnership with God. Here is her testimony in her own words:

> *I began working with Linda in June of 2012 at a really difficult time in my life, both personally and professionally. Linda's gift of compassion was clear as she listened to my*

concerns and offered useful strategies that have all proven to be very effective. It is now January 2013 and as I reflect on our journey together, I realize God placed Linda in my pathway to lead me back to Him. Her series, "Find Your Why Forward" has helped me to better understand the immense love God has for me no matter what situation I find myself in. The journey continues with the peace of knowing I am here to serve God and as Linda shares, "You will see your vision become more clear, your leadership will rise up, your joy will burst out, you will be doing what you were made to do, in God's strength."

This transformation in my client would not have occurred had I gone in with my own agenda. Instead, I was simply following the leading of God as my Chief Consultant.

What results can we expect to see?

When Leader-Believers carry God's presence into the workplace we will see angry customers taken care of well, impatient bosses calmed, urgent deadlines reached with composure, work done with excellence and team members treated with respect and love. Moses' face was shining after He went up to the mountain to talk with God (Exod. 34:30). In the early church, Peter and John preached the gospel with great confidence and stunning results despite their lack of education and training. Their observers were amazed and recognized them as having been with Jesus (Acts 4:13-14). We too should bear evidence in our countenance and actions of having been with Him.

The fulfillment of the desire for impact that lies at the core of our being is found in partnering with the God who made us and has strategically placed us in specific spheres of influence and in certain assignments. As we partner with our God and begin to flow in His love, we find ourselves teaching and training the ones around us. Someone once said to me, "The world needs to see Jesus with skin on." Is that our cloak? Are we reflecting Jesus "with skin on?" Wearing one "seamless robe"[xvii] at home, at work and in the community where we bring God's presence with us in all we do brings clarity of mind, quiets the conflict of the soul and launches us into being a part of the restoration story. Each life restored, each heart acknowledged, each business day where we have blessed one another, each new opportunity to know our God is another day in the unfolding of the restoration all creation longs for.

Engage with the Holy

Partnering with God for Impact

Dear Lord God,

I love that You are a God of love. Fill me by Your Spirit with the "love that surpasses comprehension" (Eph. 3:19), and I will engage Your heart to love others. I want to work in partnership with You to love my family, friends, coworkers and everyone that I encounter as I go about my daily work, teaching and training others along the way.

Let me not lose sight of Your partnership with me, for it is only through You I will make a deep and lasting impact on the lives of others. Today I choose to inquire of You, run with You, and respond to Your divine leadership. Jesus, I want to love You back and watch as You love others through me.

Thank you for the divine privilege to know Your love as You fill me again this day.

In Jesus Name,

Signed:

Date

Chapter 4
The Where: Your Spheres of Influence

God has done all this, so that we will look for him and reach out and find him. He isn't far from any of us.
(Acts 17:27, CEV)

Partnership with God brings us into new realms of impact potential. We are working in love, ready to teach and train others, but exactly how and where? God's strategy for our lives invites us to participate in His greatness, and we must find an arena for the expression of this greatness (or we shall explode!). We are born to release the greatness of God in the context of the world. We are called to *be* the church in all of society rather than just go to church. In the landscape of life, we engage with other people to carry out the business of living. God has placed us in a specific context, time and place to carry a certain influence. He has called us to be the church in that context. He uses men and women like us to put the church on display to those around us.

God's attention to detail is amazing to consider. He is the grand strategist with a plan that encompasses nations yet reaches individual people. We will look at three types of spheres of influence as we explore His ways.

Firstly we will look at the spheres of time and place together, which invite us to reach for and find God. This arena sets the stage for us to begin functioning as Leader-Believers.

Secondly we will study spheres of society where we express the God that we have found to others. This section accounts for a majority of this chapter as we delve into the understanding of our arenas of expression. Some might call these classrooms or platforms where we function.

Thirdly we will address spheres of authority governing the reach of our impact as we share God's presence in society. These spheres serve as guardrails, providing a safety zone where we are to focus our lives and work.

As we unpack these three types of spheres, I encourage you to develop a comprehensive view and resist the tendency to camp out in any one area at the expense of the others. You need an informed understanding that will equip you to work optimally in your spheres of influence.

Recently a young woman I am mentoring sent me a text for Mother's Day. The first text said: "Hell Mama Fields, Happy Mother's Day!" In her haste to greet me and wish me a blessed Mother's Day, the message was incomplete and resulted in a rather humorous and entirely different message from the one she intended. The next text said: "Meant to say Hello Mama Fields…"

When we strike out to do God's work too quickly or prematurely, we often channel our enthusiasm and energy wrongly at the expense of our impact for Christ. We want to operate from a complete strategy in issuing blessings to our spheres of influence. Let's work with the revelation we have from God and become Leader-Believers who exemplify Christ in our spheres of influence.

Spheres of Time and Place

> *And He has made from one blood every nation of men to dwell on all the face of the earth, and has determined their preappointed times and the boundaries of their dwellings, so that they should seek the Lord, in the hope that they might grope for Him and find Him, though He is not far from each one of us. (Acts 17:26-27)*

At every level the Lord has our fellowship with Him at the heart of His strategies; even the times, seasons and places where God has placed us individually and corporately serve to lead us to Him. You have probably heard it said that "timing is everything." When you deliver a sales presentation in answer to a potential client's need of services, you experience the benefits of good timing by delivering a solution at just the right time. On God's timeline, we find that nations and the people in them are placed within those boundaries at certain moments in history by His plan. The sons of Issachar are known in the Bible for understanding the times and the seasons, specifically "to know what Israel ought to do" (1 Chron. 12:32). There was a recognized relationship between the times and a strategy for the country. God is working out a plan from salvation to restoration that includes intentional timing in His placement of men and nations.

You've also heard it said that business success is all about "location, location, location" – acknowledging the importance of being at the *right* place. God's intricate strategy for shaping men and nations through geographical placement all began when He spoke the world into existence and placed Adam and Eve in the garden to have fellowship with Him. Over time, God has made every nation to dwell on the earth within specific geographic boundaries.

When we realize God's plan is complete and includes the specific details of our lives, it enhances our appreciation of our impact in a particular place and time. Reflecting on the different places I have lived, I can identify unique invitations to find God in every location. Think about your own life and circumstances and how you have found the Lord or become aware of His presence in various settings. I visited the church of my childhood recently, and memories of Mrs. Sanders, Mrs. Tillman and many other wise saints telling the stories of Jesus flooded my mind as I walked the halls of the Sunday school classrooms. Standing in the sanctuary, I could envision my dad preaching in the pulpit and my Mom singing in the choir, wearing her turquoise choir robe. In this little town of Lytle, Texas, when I was a mere child, my parents and the church members provoked me to learn about Jesus.

Later, in college, I began to speak to young people at camps and in churches at the urging of my leaders and peers. I can name several examples of people God placed in my life in certain situations who guided me by their words and examples on what became my path to training and teaching. My eccentric boss and Economics Professor, Dr. Morgan, encouraged me to become a Graduate Assistant and get my MBA right after graduating with my bachelor's. I did. I officed next door to my mentor, Dr. Chiodo, who was a living example of bringing God's presence to the students, and I fell in love with college teaching in the Hill Country of Texas at an appointed place and time. Granted, this is my personal micro application of Acts 17:26-27; what is yours?

Once we have found God, it is natural that our influence will begin to spill over to the places where we live and work. What a Master Planner He is!

Spheres of Society

Next, we will identify the spheres of society where we bring what we have received to others. In the 70's two leaders of significant ministries received a word from the Lord which has focused much attention on the different spheres of society. The boundaries in this case refer not to geographical locations or times but to cultural spheres of influence. The year was 1975, and Bill Bright, founder of Campus Crusade, and Loren Cunningham, founder of YWAM, each had a divine appointment with God. Although they didn't know they were in the same location, these men had each decided to take some time to pray in the mountains of Colorado. Each was impressed by God to write a list of seven areas of culture and to see these areas as significant opportunities to reach people for the Lord. Through a park ranger, they connected for a visit and went on to compare notes on their time with the Lord. To their amazement, God had simultaneously given each of them the very same message.

> *This is the way to reach America and nations for God. And [God said],* "**You have to see them [the seven spheres] like classrooms or like places that were already there, and go into them with those who are already working in those areas.**" *Three weeks later, Dr. Francis Shaffer... on TV had the same list! And so I realized that this was for the body of Christ. These areas were: Religion, Family, Education, Politics, Arts, Media, and Business.*[xviii]

Why do I love this account so much? It is to me much like Moses going up the mountain and hearing from God a fresh revelation for our day and time in history!

Later, YWAM updated the list of spheres to read:

Economy (business, science and technology)
Education
Family
Government
Celebration (sports, entertainment, and art)

Media
Religion

Regardless of the terminology, we know that God desires to work in *every* sphere of culture. God referred to familiar areas of life to remind us to take the church out among those "who are already there." Being the church in the places where we spend time every day brings the presence of God into the city rather than trying to bring the city into the church. "This is the way to reach America and the world for God." We have wrongly defined evangelism when we forget to live our Christianity in the places God has positioned us; we cannot effectively invite others into a life we do not live ourselves. Let's carefully pay attention to what these fathers in the faith heard from the Lord. Their message has greatly motivated many Leader-Believers to take their societal roles more seriously.

"Spheres are like classrooms" – the classroom analogy is powerful and applies to every sphere of society. Each sphere represents a classroom waiting for a teacher. When no Leader-Believer comes to the front of the class, someone else will step forward to fill the leadership vacuum.

Many Christians are already in place as leaders and decision-makers in all spheres of society, but have yet to grasp the connection between what happens on Sunday and what they do on Monday. They have been physically present but not spiritually present in their work.[xix]

➔**KEY**: Cast vision for transformation; raise the bar.

In Proverbs 29:18 we read, "Where there is no vision, the people perish."

When Leader-Believers cast vision in their spheres of influence, others are greatly encouraged to live the Christian life outside the walls of the church building. I had the opportunity to provide business consulting in Bulgaria and found eager business leaders ready to grow and learn how to advance their businesses. They were familiar with Christian principles, but lived as if they applied only at church on the weekend. I found that their Christian values did not carry over into business transactions when the work week began because their culture did not allow for doing business without a bribe. Bribery was the norm. Leader-Believers had not made inroads to bring their values to the front of the Economy sphere or "classroom." They needed encouragement to pray and to apply their Christian values in their work. Energized with the challenge of living their beliefs every day of the week, these leaders were ready to take a step towards the front of the Economy classroom and begin the journey of transforming the business culture.

→ **KEY**: Go to the head of the class.

Sphere of Authority - The Measure of your Sphere

We are responsible for the measure of the sphere where God has placed us in our work, our cities and communities. As we apply this principle, we would be wise to view the limits of our authority in order to understand our responsibility accurately. Paul addresses his area of influence as he speaks of his ministry:

> *But we will not boast beyond limits, but will boast only with regard to the area of influence God assigned to us, to reach even to you. For we are not overextending ourselves… (2 Cor. 10:13-14a, ESV)*

Overextending ourselves results when we go beyond the authority we have been given as a leader or an employee. We are wise to run in our own power alley with the assignment we have been given.

Often people ask me how they can function as a Leader-Believer in their jobs if they are not the head of the company or if they don't work in a Christian-owned company. One Christian business owner I know has a room set aside where employees can come in and spend time in prayer during the workday. In this company, the values are based on Christian principles and the prayer room is a clear signal that this is a Christian company. The leaders value prayer and demonstrate that value by praying about the direction of the company, employees and customers.

Others I know are employed in a company that is not necessarily owned by Christians; they are individual contributors whose sphere is perhaps only the cubicle where they work. What can they do? They can pray as they work, and ask the Lord to bless coworkers and customers, working within the sphere of authority right where they are.

Much spiritual authority is in the hands of the janitor praying while he cleans the building, the clerk blessing the customers in a shop, the Christian cook flipping hamburgers with a smile, and the project director who treats his team with kindness. The spiritual authority given empowers each one working in his own lane or power alley to work unto the Lord; this action brings transformation.

On the other hand, Leader-Believers can be reluctant to lead even within the sphere they live and work in for a variety of reasons. What keeps leaders back?

People sit on the sidelines for many reasons: a lack of vision, a compartmentalized view of society and the roles in which we serve, the fact that we have become accustomed to waiting on someone "in charge" to lead the way or invite us to take the stage. We have often relegated vision-casting to a deputized position and have many dormant vision casters sitting with the students in the classroom. Can you picture an adult sitting in a child's desk? This is the mental picture I get when I think of all the gifted people waiting for an assignment or an invitation to contribute their vision. They are already qualified and able to lead, yet ever sitting in the

student desk with their knees crammed under their chins, waiting to be called on.

→ **KEY**: Don't sit on the sidelines. Lead now.

Lack of vision for the workplace as a valid Christian calling is the number one reason I hear that people do not fully engage in their workplace. One solution is to alert individuals to the fact that the workplace puts them next to those who need prayer, who need to see a Christian doing excellent work, and who may want to learn more about God. Vision of what it means to bring God's presence in the workplace validates the Leader-Believer even in the small mundane tasks that must be done.

→ **KEY**: Get a clear vision.

The water-cooler conversation, the report completed on time, the excellence of our words and work are all valid ways to show God's goodness in the workplace. These examples are as important as the healing prayer for a sick coworker or the encouragement of a downhearted team member. The Leader-Believer who works "as unto the Lord" is not prone to disconnect their work lives from their Christian values. Values are made evident by the way we live in all aspects of our lives.

→ **KEY**: How we live speaks louder than what we say.

A pulse check should reveal where we need to bring our beliefs and actions into alignment so that we are speaking and living the same reality, bringing God's presence as we work.

A wrong view of leadership looks down on Christians who advance. It implies that it is not godly to advance, lead, make money, or be successful. Therefore many fall into a poverty mindset financially and professionally. To flourish in our calling and sphere is not only fulfilling to the individual Leader-Believer, but attractive to others looking for role models of success. Good leadership attracts followers who want to follow in your steps. God has made us in His image; He loves and enjoys us and has put us on display to the world to show off His great love and bring others into it. We are God's "image-bearers," creating restoration as we work.

The Lord has provided us the parable of the talents in Luke 19:11-27 to teach us that He expects us to invest the gifts He has provided us. God gives His people gifts, talents, and resources to use and multiply. In this parable, the nobleman dispersed silver to the servants and gave instructions to invest what they had been entrusted with.

> *Before he left, he called together ten of his servants and divided among them ten pounds of silver, saying, "Invest this for me while I am gone." (Luke 19:13, NLT)*

When the nobleman returned, he called them together to hear a report of their results. He rewarded the servants according to what they did with what he had given them. Those who invested the silver and multiplied it were given authority over cities. He was greatly disappointed to find that one had done absolutely nothing with his silver. The Lord expects us to be faithful to use our gifts and multiply the investment.

➔ **KEY:** Invest your gifts and create your story.

Leader-Believer Stories

Here are a few examples of individuals who stepped into their calling as Leader-Believers in their spheres of influence. These people did not wait to be called as full-time clergy to bring change in their worlds. They simply loved God, heard His leading, and then obeyed Him in the place where He had strategically positioned them. They responded to God and walked with Him in partnership, and have changed their environments remarkably.

Real Estate Success in the Economy Sphere

Diane Bickle started Glad Heart Realty for two specific reasons: to serve people relocating to Kansas City to be a part of the International House of Prayer and to help fund the ministry through the sale of those homes. The stated purpose of the company is as follows:

> "Glad Heart Realty's express purpose is to serve our clientele with care and skill as unto the Lord while we serve the IHOP-KC missions base in a wholehearted way, which includes our corporate profit," relays Diane. "We hold weekly prayer meetings as a company and pray for God's purposes to be made manifest in our city, our own lives and those of our clients."[xx]

Leadership by Diane, the Manager Broker, provides a system other real estate professionals can plug into who share the same vision. Glad Heart Realty has contributed over one million dollars to the prayer movement.

Fashion Industry Success

Gloria Kim, owner of an international contemporary fashion company called JOYPEACE, credits God as being her financier, her Chief Consultant and her daily partner in business. Gloria creates clothing with edifying messages printed across the front of the shirts such as, "Anything is Possible."

Gloria keeps a piano keyboard in her office for worship throughout the day. Early each morning, she goes to God and "frames the day" in prayer. She prays an anointing over every shipment that goes out across the world, that those who buy and wear the clothing pieces will feel God's presence. JOYPEACE has made significant inroads in the fashion apparel market as a refreshing contrast to the lines of darkness and death attracting many young people.

Godly Influence in the Governmental Realm

Governmental leaders influence constituents of their state or country. Their actions are noted by the people they govern. Leaders such as these have encouraged believers by calling for prayer. Governor Brownback of Kansas called a prayer meeting for the country on the grounds of the state capitol. Governor Rick Perry of Texas held a prayer meeting for those who wanted to seek God for their leaders. Abraham Lincoln was a man of prayer. When leaders in government seek God, believers are encouraged to pray in their own realms of influence.

Because governmental leaders are in the limelight, their actions, campaigns and beliefs come under the scrutiny of the public eye. An unorthodox campaign became the story of Dr. Saviour Chishimba, who rose through the ranks of education in Zambia to head an NGO. He ran for a parliamentary seat and, rather than rely on the traditional campaign methods his competitors used, he simply preached the gospel in every region.

Six parliamentary candidates ran for the Kasama Central seat; Saviour won by a landslide. While in office, the Lord directed him to address corruption in the government. God used Dr. Chishimba's voice to raise a standard.

Character Building in Education

My mentor and university professor, Dr. Beverly Chiodo, dramatically influenced my life and career. She cast vision for her students who were all future business men and women by teaching them to acknowledge honorable character traits in those who had impacted their lives. In her communications class she had the students write letters thanking those who had impacted them for the better. Her list of character traits was taken from the Bible. She was teaching character development in a public university in a way that provoked a younger generation to impact others' lives simply by highlighting the effects of leaders in their own lives.

God in the Media

Without finance, recognition or institutional backing, Rory and Wendy Alec launched the first daily Christian television network in Great Britain and Europe from a kitchen table on the outskirts of London in 1995. Today the GOD TV Network broadcasts to an incredible 437 million viewers in over 200 nations across the world... and now to screens across the Direct TV platform in North America. Their story, *Against All Odds*, chronicles the journey of their TV ministry from dream to reality.

Becoming Family

Randy Bohlender, founder of the Zoe Foundation, has such a love for family that not only has he adopted several children, but he helps others do the same. He formed the Zoe Foundation to help fund adoptions and promote a positive alternative to abortion (www.thezoefoundation.com).

Sports

Whether a small town football team gathers for prayer before the game or an NFL quarterback kneels alone after a touchdown, many Leader-Believer sports figures love to give credit to God for their victories. They have intertwined their love of God and sports and often bring God's presence to their locker rooms and playing fields by thanking Him for their abilities.

Religion: Mobilizing Marketplace Leader-Believers from the Pulpit

One of the most powerful ministries needed in the earth today is the launch of marketplace Leader-Believers from the pulpit. As pastors and religious leaders embrace and bless men and women in the marketplace, many in the church body will receive healing from fractured identities – healing which will have significant repercussions. Not only will marketplace professionals hold their heads up as they walk in their sacred callings, but they will come to the table in church circles not only as financial contributors, but as visionaries, laborers and cohesive strategists with answers the church desperately needs.

I personally appreciate the blessings that flow from those who work full-time in the sphere of religion, beginning with my father and my earlier pastors, Ernie James and Scott McKay. They cheered me on as I created the corporate learning center and drew upon the testimony of what God was doing by embracing my gifts and talents in the church. Scott had me bring this blessing to the congregation through speaking, leading task forces and implementing small group ministry. Mike Bickle so values the role of those working in all spheres of society that he has made a place in the ministry of the International House of Prayer in Kansas City for men and women in the marketplace to be trained through The Joseph Company, which I am privileged to lead. When religious leaders proclaim destiny over those on the front lines of society, they mobilize God's army in all spheres of influence.

My Assignment

Reflecting on my own experience of creating and running a corporate learning center in Texas, I remember having the sense that God had presented me with an assignment. The prayer on the legal tablet never left my mind. As I engaged with the Holy in my professional life I found God helping me lead the charge with confidence, bringing great results.

He was right with me as I assessed situations, defined the need and created out-of-the-box solutions. When I stepped into this role, I knew I would work harder than I had ever worked. I simultaneously knew I was learning lessons that could be applied on a much broader scale by many other Leader-Believers if only they would step into the divine partnership and work with God.

I found the thrill of creating an entrepreneurial corporate training center drew on my people skills, demanded accurate business analysis and required problem solving skills; to my delight I pioneered new territory. I knew only one way to hire and manage people, execute projects and deliver dynamic results in training and human performance – and that was the way of prayer. Many times I asked God if I should be in full-time ministry, and His answer was:

"Yes, and you are in full-time ministry."

I have filled many prayer journals with questions I asked the Lord in this process and the answers that came. I saw employees meet God and learn to trust Him. Many received a new and personal understanding of Jesus Christ. Others were healed of hurting hearts.

As a result of viewing my opportunity in business and education as a way to touch lives for the Lord, I often prayed for my team before getting to the office each day. I wanted to be able to bless them and encourage them. As the Holy Spirit would guide me, I would help each one to work through problems in the context of our professional lives. It came quite naturally and was not contrived or superficial.

In getting to know one of the star players on our team, Lynda, I came to understand that there was a significant burden in her life resulting from the tragedy of having lost a child some years back. One day she opened up to share a little about the experience with me, and I led her in a simple prayer for Jesus to heal her pain. The next day, Lynda rushed into my office and quickly shut the door. She turned around and excitedly began to tell me how the Lord had healed her great pain in the night while she was asleep. She said, "Jesus knew He had to do it while I was asleep because the pain was so great I couldn't have stood it otherwise. God's presence came over my entire body and literally lifted all the grief and hurt out of my heart. I have never felt anything like this and the pain is gone!"

The business endeavor I was leading resulted not only in changed lives on my team, but in tremendous economic development in our region. In my own career and life, I took a divine assignment in education and business and did it God's way.

Sphere of Time and Place

Why did I take this journey with God? I was intrigued with the geographic location and the specific challenges and needs of the Brazoria County at the time. I believed that God brought me to the Brazosport area for specific reasons and I wanted to know them and fulfill His plans in partnership with the Holy Spirit.

Sphere of Society

I was paying attention to the spheres of Education and Business as I am drawn to these areas and gifted for them.

My leadership had matured through my years of being faithful in the college classroom and doing well with programs I had been entrusted to lead in the fields of marketing, banking and economic development.

Sphere of Authority

I had been promoted to Director over the new opportunity I had prayed for on that yellow legal tablet. I was aware that the assignments in front of me were far more than earning a paycheck.

My assignment represented a specific opportunity in a geographical location at a point in time which would be realized through the societal realms of education and business.

Getting to know God was my top priority; it is the one most important thing I am after in my lifetime. On this course, God has revealed His strategies as I work time after time. Like Dr. Chiodo, I found that clients represented divine invitations to bring the presence of God into their lives. Like Diane Bickle, I valued the resource we were creating for the community. Like Wendy and Rory Alec, I spent hours pouring over plans at my dining room table, asking for God to provide solutions.

This opportunity to partner with the Lord was the culmination of many assignments and prayers over the span of many years for me, as it is for many other Leader-Believers willing to hear the challenge – and take it. The assignments span all spheres of society and will change over time, and the faces of many characters will come across the landscape of our lives. Challenges will present themselves, and victories will be sweet. All these facets of life provide opportunity and circumstance to get to know God in each new situation. As believers look around and recognize they are already in classrooms, they will begin to show up for class fully engaged.

Each of us have opportunity to engage with God and engage with our customers, students, coworkers, and the public at large in a way that brings God's presence to the situation. As teachers step onto their platforms while other believers deliver influence from the back of the room, we can expect more results that reflect God's ways and impact the seven spheres of society in greater measure.

We are the Church

The church is the body of Christ in relation to one another. The Great Commission extends beyond a decision for salvation. Salvation is the beginning, and partnering with God to bring restoration seven days a week where we are is the on-going reality of our salvation. One of the reasons I found success in my career is that I did not cease to pray about my work just because it happened outside the walls of a church building. Quite the contrary, prayer is what sustained me and guided me to make wise hiring decisions, build innovative programs, build a high performance team and run with excellence. Many staff members came to me at different times expressing fulfillment at being in an atmosphere where I was concerned for their growth as individuals. They acknowledged the importance of prayer because they felt the effects of it in their personal and professional lives. I often voiced a prayer prior to key presentations, asking for God to help us. We prayed for sick staff members, broken hearts and guidance in their lives along the way. I did not make a public display of prayer or hang out a sign, but people knew where to come for a supportive prayer in time of need. The church is expressed by the saints dispersed throughout all spheres of culture. In which sphere(s) are you being the church?

Picture a teacher speaking a blessing over a sick child. Imagine a businessman praying over a customer as he has opportunity to encourage them. Think of a city council member networking with other believers and praying over the city. Envision believers on a school board implementing a school system in a Christ-like manner which blesses teachers and students alike.

Your ministry is worked out in all the different aspects of your life:

Are you a cook? Are you a checker?

Are you a teacher, professor, or administrator?

Maybe you are a lawyer? A judge? A doctor?

Do you working in a business? Perhaps you are an entrepreneur or a philanthropist?

Do you work as a mayor or City Council representative?

Is your profession that of a writer, entertainer or producer?

In each individual life and assignment, Christians are called to change the spiritual landscape of the earth by bringing God's presence in their own job, company and location within the sphere of their authority.

Your Sphere of Influence

What sphere(s) of influence are you involved in? God has His people strategically positioned in all arenas of culture today. To ignore your role is to pass up an opportunity for partnership with God. At the same time, you don't want to reach beyond your sphere. Your mantle of leadership, as we will explore in a later chapter, will reveal your voice and your reach in your sphere. Let us realize our high calling and pray that we may bring the very presence of God into the world.

Engage with the Holy

Thriving in my Sphere(s) of Influence

Dear Lord God,

Thank You that I am called to impact the sphere of influence right where You have placed me. Forgive me for trying to plan a great escape from the very place You appointed for me to thrive in partnership with You. You have known me and planned for me all the days of my life.

1. Show me how to embrace You in the geographical boundary of my dwelling and work at this specific time.

2. I acknowledge my involvement in these spheres of society:

3. Reveal to me how to bring Your presence in the sphere of authority you have allotted to me now.

Lord, this partnership with You is so wonderful I want others to have it too. Show me how to bring Your presence one person at a time, one decision at a time, in my assigned place.

Help me recognize and appreciate Your leadership in my life. Thank You for Your great attention to my life.

Now use me in greater ways, Lord.

In Jesus Name,

Signed:

Date:

Chapter 5
The Who: Your Custom Leadership Mantle

> *Remember your leaders, those who spoke to you the word of God. Consider the outcome of their way of life, and imitate their faith. (Heb. 13:7, ESV)*

Spheres of influence define your invitation to bring impact with your voice through your work at a particular time and place in society. However, a key element of success for Leader-Believers will be the credibility with which they influence their realm of authority.[xxi] Just as the teacher influences the classroom, Leader-Believers have the opportunity to influence the spheres where they live and work. Influence is the capacity to have an effect on the character, development, or behavior of someone or something. Other words we use for influence include impact, authority, and action.[xxii]

> ➔ **KEY**: Leader-Believers deliver impact by taking credible action in their realm of authority.

Good leaders model the principles of leadership. A good leader will bring about a certain outcome by his example through a cause and effect relationship.

My friend Maciej Woloski is a successful CFO of multiple companies in Poland. He plans his day in prayer. As Maciej says, "If you don't plan your day, something or someone else will plan it for you. If you don't start your day with your own liturgy unto God, you will be influenced rather than being an influencer."

→ **KEY**: Take personal responsibility and learn about your
Mantle of Leadership.

Designing your Custom Leadership Mantle is the primary focus of this chapter as we dive into valuable lessons from the examples of some of the most incredible leaders of the Bible. In the following pages, you will specifically want to note lessons to implement as well as pitfalls to avoid as you begin to explore how to create your own custom Mantle of Leadership. Take note of the keys and qualities you want and need as we examine different Leadership Mantles. This will equip you to describe your own development plan to become a better leader in this season of your life. Remember that everyone is a leader to someone whether you lead the kids next door by your daily example, the soccer team you coach, the class you teach, or a corporation you own or work in. We all want to be the best leaders we can be. Think about your current assignment and the challenges you face. You will reference the qualities you want to focus on when we get to the final section where you assemble your own Leadership Mantle. Now, let's take a closer look at the lives of a few biblical leaders to see how they impacted situations and people by moving in their authority and wearing well their Mantles of Leadership.

The Mantle of Authority: Elijah anoints Elisha for Leadership

> *So he departed from there and found Elisha the son of Shaphat, while he was plowing with twelve pairs of oxen before*

*him, and he with the twelfth. And Elijah passed over to him
and threw his mantle on him. (1 Kings 19:19, NASB)*

Elijah had been instructed by the Lord to anoint Elisha as
prophet in his place. When Elijah found Elisha plowing in a
field, he threw his mantle over him, signifying the passing of
his own leadership anointing to Elisha. An actual cloak was
passed to Elisha as a physical representation of a spiritual
invitation to become Elijah's successor.

What happened during the time preceding Elisha's
commencement as Elijah's successor? The process included
far more than Elijah tossing a cloak over his protégé. What
happened next can be characterized as a real-time internship
in Leadership School. While many things can be learned
academically, the most effective lessons are grasped in
relationship and in the context of real-life experience.

Elisha was working his job plowing the field when Elijah
encountered him, inspiring his transition to leadership school.
"An honest calling in the world does not put us out of the
way of our heavenly calling, any more than it did Elisha."[xxiii]
Elisha responded from the field to avail himself of both
dynamics – relationship and life context – when he entered
into a time of learning from his mentor, Elijah.

➔**KEY:** Go to Leadership School.

Elisha was willing to learn. In fact he was hungry to learn
from his mentor, and he signed up for Leadership School by
entering into relationship with Elijah. He was eager to receive
every morsel of training and anointing that Elijah would pass
to him. The interim period from the day Elijah's cloak fell
upon Elisha to the day his master was taken up into heaven
must have encompassed times of prayer, fasting, operating in
the prophetic and many 'regular' days. Mentor and protégé
became so close that we find Elisha unwilling to leave Elijah's

side as his time of departure drew near. He placed himself in the teacher's path.

→ **KEY**: Sign up hungry.

Elisha studied and walked with Elijah, leaving his own family and land behind. In serving Elijah, Elisha was bringing himself under the tutelage of his master. When we serve another leader, we enlist in one of the highest forms of training by taking the lowest possible road. Making copies in the back room, setting up the travel schedule and sitting in on meetings provide unique times for leader and protégé to work together, and for valuable lessons to emerge. This is the place where organic behind-the-scenes mentoring occurs.

→ **KEY**: Train by serving.

On the day that Elijah ascended into heaven, Elisha was present and embraced his assignment. He even asked for a double portion of his mentor's spirit when presented the opportunity. Would we be found with a ready answer at such a moment in time? Elisha was ready because he had already set his heart to absorb every possible teaching and impartation from Elijah.

> *When they had crossed over, Elijah said to Elisha, "Ask what I shall do for you before I am taken from you." And Elisha said, "Please, let a double portion of your spirit be upon me." (2 Kings 2:9)*

Elisha's schooling was complete and his actions began to reveal greater power and anointing.

> *[13] He also took up the mantle of Elijah that fell from him and returned and stood by the bank of the Jordan. [14] He took the mantle of Elijah that fell from him and struck the waters and said, "Where is the LORD, the God of Elijah?" And when he*

IMPACT Your Sphere of INFLUENCE

also had struck the waters, they were divided here and there;
and Elisha crossed over. [15] Now when the sons of the prophets
who were at Jericho opposite him saw him, they said, "The
spirit of Elijah rests on Elisha." And they came to meet him
and bowed themselves to the ground before him."
(2 Kings 2:13-15, NASB)

➔**KEY**: Let the evidence speak.

When Elisha divided the waters, he was recognized as having
been with Elijah by those who saw him operating in increased
power. He was walking out his calling, moving in increased
authority and demonstrating the call on his life. Although this
moment cannot be forced, there is a time to put what we
have learned into practice. We want to remain teachable and
continue to grow as we move from our Leadership School
internship to our next assignment.

Leadership Lessons for the Mantle of Authority

Current day leaders also develop by serving other leaders, and
over time the evidence of such training emerges through the
fruit of our ministries and work. We make ourselves available
to learn when we say "yes" and sign up for Leadership School
by serving other leaders.

Let's agree to receive our own Mantle of Leadership. Isaiah
61:3 speaks of a "garment of praise" where the garment
represents a posture or an attitude of praise. In the same way,
think of the mantle as a posture or virtual uniform. Just as
you recognize a pilot by his uniform which indicates his
authority to fly a plane, you carry a certain presence signifying
your leadership and ability to carry out your particular
assignment. Don't expect to live a life just like Elisha, but
please consider the invitation to accept your own custom
Mantle of Leadership which is just your size, just your style
and perfect for training in what God has called you to do.

Let's look at the steps involved in assembling your mantle and some pitfalls to avoid in this part of your Leadership School.

1. Trust God for your leadership development. You will wonder at times, "How does my mantle look?" When you live and work as you wear your mantle of leadership, your actions will demonstrate some level of your calling. A word of caution here: your mantle should not become your focal point. It simply represents a decision to say "yes" to the leadership which God has invited you to walk in as you carry out your life assignments. A wise approach is to seek God for your leadership development and listen to sound counsel. Look to serve mentors and stay in communication with others who are doing what you aspire to do, and your mantle will be established. On the surface you may think that nothing is happening, but quite the reverse is true. When you find yourself in an unseen place, this is often where the most important lessons occur, shaping you for what is to come.

2. Take the low road. You will need to learn to walk in humility commensurate with your role as a leader. There will always be hurdles to surmount as you learn how to respond to disappointment or perhaps even betrayal. The saying "No pain, no gain" applies here. Serving the vision of others in humility is a proving ground where the Lord offers to teach leaders how to truly serve.

3. Remember, your development is a process. When you find yourself wondering, "Are we there yet?" you will want to recall that your identity as a leader is being shaped throughout your life experience. This is a hopeful prospect for us because it reminds us that

God is interested in developing leaders over the
course of our lives. In Chapter 6 we will explore the
Leader-Believer development process in greater detail
and examine the stages of maturity we each
pass through.

Pitfalls to Avoid: Whining

Some may ask, "What if others do not recognize me as a
leader?" The answer to this is that you are still in training.
Do not worry about whether others recognize your
leadership; rather begin to serve in any way possible, no
matter how small or insignificant it may seem. Serve others
and become more concerned with competently completing
the tasks God has placed before you than with who is
watching. Remember as well that you will never become
greater in public than you are in private. On the platform or
in your leadership role you will not suddenly become a person
of humility with a great message if you haven't cultivated a
humble heart while cleaning out offices or doing the behind-
the-scenes work. If you have a message of encouragement for
others in need when you are the janitor, you may well have
one when you are president of the company. I often think of
the stories my dad told of his job mopping the floors at the
seminary while he studied to become a pastor. Years later at
his funeral, accomplished men with patents to their names
who had stood before presidents wept as they spoke of
desiring to walk in the humility they saw in my dad.

A Mantle of Leadership is developed by the influence of
other leaders. Some you will serve directly and work with,
others you will read about and some you will watch from a
distance. Don't panic if you do not find yourself with a direct
mentor like Elisha did. Over the years, many have lamented
to me that they would have given anything to have a Dad like
mine. My reply is always, "Take his story and learn from
him." Don't be deterred, God is your teacher. The Lord's

leadership supersedes our circumstances. Our job is to have a hunger for learning, a willingness to serve and be trained, and the obedience to demonstrate our calling in due time.

Let's look at other examples in the Bible where individuals adapted a posture to learn and accepted a mantle to lead. As you progress, you have the opportunity to customize your own Mantle of Leadership as God reveals the elements needed for your unique Leadership School in this season. Highlight the things that stand out to you. Your mantle will speak of your unique characteristics and personality, but remember that you will also find the need to develop new aspects of leadership in different situations as you grow in impact and influence. Leadership School is not static, but rather a dynamic experience.

The Mantle of the Marketplace and Worship: Lydia, Sales Professional

We know two things about Lydia. First, her professional role was in sales; she was a seller of purple. The area of Thyatira was famous for the manufacture and use of purple dye, and Lydia had brought this business to Philippi.[xxiv] Second, she was a worshiper of God. We find her in a house of prayer where others gathered on the Sabbath.

> [13] *And on the Sabbath day we went outside the gate to a riverside, where we were supposing that there would be a place of prayer; and we sat down and began speaking to the women who had assembled.* [14] *A woman named Lydia, from the city of Thyatira, a seller of purple fabrics, a worshiper of God, was listening; and the Lord opened her heart to respond to the things spoken by Paul.* [15] *And when she and her household had been baptized, she urged us, saying, "If you have judged me to be faithful to the Lord, come into my house and stay." And she prevailed upon us. (Acts 16:13-15, NASB)*

→ **KEY**: Be a worshiper of God.

After the Lord opened her heart to the gospel she became the first convert in Europe. Lydia was a woman of influence and her family and servants followed her example in professing faith and being baptized. Did this include employees or servants in the business as well as family? It appears that Lydia intertwined her business and spiritual life together as a worshiper and a praying woman.

→ **KEY**: The Marketplace Mantle transfers to the ministry team.

She even persuaded the little prayer group to meet at her house. We find later that Lydia had become a close-knit member of the band of believers when Paul was released from jail and came to her house.

They went out of the prison and entered the house of Lydia, and when they saw the brethren, they encouraged them and departed.
(Acts 16:40, NASB)

Lydia was found faithful in her business and her ministry. She is not referenced many times in the Scripture, but we can imagine what her life my have looked like. What was Lydia's calling card as she traveled the road to market where potential buyers would analyze her purple dyes and plan to negotiate her to a bottom-line price? As she met merchants, how did she introduce herself? "Welcome to the Market at Philippi. I am Lydia and you can view the finest purple money can buy at my shop. Be sure you come by to see the rich dyes we have brought from Thyatira. I am a seller of purple and a worshiper of the one true God."

→ **KEY**: Develop your elevator speech.

We do know from the Scripture that she was a woman of action. Let's learn from Lydia's example.

Leadership Lessons for the Mantle of the Marketplace and Worship

1. Execute creative ideas to completion. Lydia was an accomplished business person. She new how to close the loop, dot the "i" and cross the "t." She demonstrated her execution skills by bringing a product to market.

2. Bring work skills to the table. Lydia's marketplace skills and experience equipped her to be a quick study in Paul's group of believers. They found her ready to bring solutions, open her home, and bring others with her.

3. Mind the home front. Lydia cared for her family first. As soon as she believed, she brought her whole household into the faith. She worked in the most important sphere of influence available to any leader, her own home (the sphere of family), and most likely among her servants in the business as well. Often men and women can overlook the sphere of influence in their own houses and shops while aspiring to do great things for God in the earth.

4. Be a trusted team player. Lydia quickly became a trusted member of the team. She volunteered what she had to offer without being invited into a specific role of authority. Lydia had a house and persuaded the worshipers to come to her home. Later we see that the disciples came to her home after being released from jail. She became a trusted supporter in times of trouble for Paul. He went to her home and encouraged the other believers there.

Pitfalls to Avoid: Making Excuses

Many look for an excuse as to why they are not moving in greater influence. In Lydia's day she could have assumed that because women in her culture did not normally rise to places of influence, she might as well not try. We don't see that behavior in Lydia; however, we do see a woman who was yielded to God in her business and her worship and who was used in the marketplace, her own home, and in the ministry of Paul.

The Mantle of Daring: Daniel

Daniel was entering the prime of his life at sixteen years of age, with dreams of his own like any young man, when his life was harshly interrupted. The Babylonians captured Daniel, separating him from his family and forcing him into an enemy's world. Daniel was emasculated and devastated of his ambitions. His name was stripped away and his very identity threatened when his new masters christened him Belteshazzar, a heathen name. When it looked like everything possible had been taken from this young man, Daniel dared to believe God for his true identity.

→**KEY:** Dare to believe God for your identity despite the critics.

After such shocking and traumatic events, when he could have been consumed with rage, Daniel reached deep within his spirit and grabbed hold of two profound connections to His true God. When Daniel found himself surrounded by a foreign culture, he dared to be different and find his identity in God against all odds.

But Daniel made up his mind that he would not defile himself with the king's choice food or with the wine which he drank; so he sought permission from the commander of the officials that he might not defile himself. (Dan. 1:8, NASB)

First, he ate differently from those around him by fasting from certain foods; second, he prayed regularly even when it was forbidden. His spiritual discipline connected him with the living God, keeping his identity intact. When Daniel dared to be different, he found that God honored his fasting and prayers with intellectual progress, spiritual favor and revelatory gifting. Daniel and his three friends were found at the head of the class when the king interviewed them after their induction period. God gave them knowledge and skill in literary studies and wisdom beyond their classmates who had eaten the standard fare of the king. Daniel also was gifted to understand visions and dreams (Dan. 1:17-20).

> ➔ **KEY**: Dare to rally praying friends.
> You need each other.

Daniel's three friends who were with him in Babylon not only dared to be different by fasting and praying with him, but they were true friends he could rally for support in the most critical times. When the king asked Daniel to interpret a dream, Daniel asked for time to prepare and immediately went to his friends to ask them to pray. Their prayers were answered as God provided the interpretation of the dream to Daniel (Dan. 2:16-19). The importance of praying friends is one of Daniel's keys to not only surviving but excelling under extreme pressure.

> ➔ **KEY**: Dare to look beyond yourself.

Daniel dared to be used by God in situations that he could have easily allowed to destroy his identity as a man of God. Instead of losing his identity, he was established as a man who knew his identity in God. Others took note and began to seek Daniel for counsel. Obviously he had divine connections and knew things they did not.

Because Daniel was established in excellence, he was hand-picked as a government official. He interpreted dreams about the rise and fall of successive kingdoms and served as a prophet during Nebuchadnezzar's reign and beyond. Instead of allowing his identity to be obliterated by the enemy, he became God's mouthpiece to kings, interpreting dreams and seeing things that would happen in the future.

Leadership Lessons for the Mantle of Daring

1. Set yourself apart to God. Do what you *can* do to set yourself apart unto God, even in the most difficult situations. Daniel identified two areas where he could do something, even as a prisoner who appeared to have lost everything. But he didn't lose the most important thing: his spiritual vibrancy. He chose to honor God with fasting and prayer.

2. Remain connected to friends especially in adversity. Daniel remained connected to three young men who were with him in captivity and who were of like mind. Bonding with other believers, especially in times of trial, lends courage to withstand tests and trials.

3. Hang on to who you are in God. Refuse to let your identity be stolen from you. Remember who you are and Whose you are. Dare to be yourself and look beyond yourself.

Pitfalls to Avoid: Giving Up

Resist the temptation to give up on your life and profession when it looks like everything has gone wrong and you seem to find yourself in the enemy's camp. Instead, dare to be different, rally praying friends, and look to retain identity in God for yourself and others.

The Mantle of a Teachable and Resilient Spirit: Esther

Esther has a phenomenal leadership story of impact as she rose from orphan to queen and savior of the Jews. The heartbreaking reality of being an orphan carries with it many obstacles of identity: loneliness, suffering, and great loss of love and belonging.

> *Father of orphans, champion of widows, is God in his holy house. God makes homes for the homeless…*
> *(Psa. 68:5-6a, MSG)*

In God's plan Esther's uncle Mordecai was in place to fill this gap as best an uncle could, and he taught her and counseled her with wisdom. But there was yet another great upset coming to Esther's young life. She was whisked away from the security of her uncle's home into a strange new environment – the king's palace. The king's wife had exhausted her job security and was being "replaced." After the decree went out for all of the young virgins to be gathered to Susa, the capital, they were placed under the watchful eye of Hegai, the king's eunuch. Once again Esther found herself in uncertainty, and once again she found a caring figure of authority waiting in Hegai.

→**KEY:** Pay attention to wise counsel.

A six month period of preparation ensued as the young women were made ready to go before the king at their appointed times. Only one would become the new queen. Esther found favor with Hegai and was advanced to the best place in the palace. When it was time for Esther to go in, she was required to choose her adornments. She could have had anything in the treasury to beautify herself in the attempt to attract the king, but she wisely sought the counsel of Hegai and took only what he advised.

Her uncle Mordecai had advised her not to reveal that she was a Jew when she entered the palace. She honored the request although it may not have made sense at the time. (Later, this move would prove to be a strategic factor in her final act to intervene on behalf of the Jews.) This young girl had learned the valuable lesson of responding to wise counsel early in life.

> *And though the Lord gives you*
> *The bread of adversity and the water of affliction,*
> *Yet your teachers will not be moved into a corner anymore,*
> *But your eyes shall see your teachers. (Isa. 30:20)*

➜ **KEY**: Respond to mentors if you want to grow past your affliction.

When tragedy robbed Esther of her family and made her an orphan, and when she was wrested from the security of her uncle's home and plunged into a dramatic contest for queen in a pagan king's palace, she landed on her feet. Her robust spirit rendered her undefeatable in the midst of huge life challenges because she was grounded in maturity beyond her age. She walked in the counsel of those who knew more than she in each new arena.

➜ **KEY**: Land on your feet; keep your footing.

A resilient spirit took Esther from orphan to queen. One of today's most highly rated skills for success in all spheres of society is the acumen to quickly adjust to new situations and constantly changing variables. Change has become our constant. Esther displayed an acute emotional agility which landed her in key positions to be used for the kingdom of God. Any one of the dramatic interruptions in her young life could easily have dealt the defeating blow, but Esther carried a robust and resilient spirit second to none.

→**KEY**: Carry yourself with a robust spirit.

Many accept the tragedy of being orphaned (literally or emotionally) as a life-time stamp upon their identity. Not this woman. She recognized and embraced her uncle Mordecai, Hegai, and eventually the king's blessing upon her young life, providing every stepping stone needed to take her from orphan to queen.

> *The king fell in love with Esther far more than with any of his other women or any of the other virgins—he was totally smitten by her. He placed a royal crown on her head and made her queen in place of Vashti. Then the king gave a great banquet for all his nobles and officials—"Esther's Banquet." He proclaimed a holiday for all the provinces and handed out gifts with royal generosity. (Est. 2:16-18, MSG)*

A feast was given in her honor: Esther's Banquet. Can you imagine what was in this woman's heart after having family wrenched from her not once but twice, to be celebrated by all the officials and servants in the land in a royal ceremony? Unbelievable favor and status rested upon this one who remained willing to adjust and grow in each daunting scenario she found herself catapulted into.

→**KEY**: Frame yourself in the big picture.

As the story of Esther unfolds, we not only see her personal rise to royal status, but her courage to face an evil plot to overthrow the Jews. Esther was a woman of fasting and prayer. Her continual response to wise counsel by God's leading took her into the palace and into a place of authority. Her personal resilience enabled her to look beyond her own plight and to that of her people.

Esther understood the larger picture, saw the strategies of the enemy and, more importantly, became the strategy of God to reverse the enemy's plans.

> → **KEY:** You may be God's strategy to
> reverse the enemy's plans.

In today's society would you like to see the reversal of evil? Would you like to discern God's plans to replace darkness with light? Are you willing to respond with resilience in different situations, as Esther did, rather than accept defeat due to your own tragedy? Will you fast and pray for the good of others?

> *And who knows whether you have not attained royalty for such a time as this? (Est. 4:14b, NASB)*

Leadership Lessons for the Mantle of a Teachable and Resilient Spirit

1. Take good advice. Being an orphan does not have to be a lifetime sentence. Look for godly mentors and those in authority you can learn from in seasons of abandonment or betrayal. God Himself is our mentor; often others are present even if for only a season. Acknowledge godly counsel and consider your timely and strategic response.

2. Come back quickly. Embrace a resilience that comes back from tragedy with the knowledge that God is present and the teachers will appear.

3. Get God's strategy. Pray and fast to understand God's strategic purposes and times beyond your own situation.

Pitfalls to Avoid: Negative Mentality

Esther had never been a queen before. When you face new opportunities resist the negative response that says, "I have never done *this* before." Rather than rehearse the things you feel disqualify you from *this* opportunity, go ahead and pray the, "But my God can do anything" prayer. God brought you here and He has a plan. Replace fear with faith to push the envelope in God's ways and time. If not now, then when will you move beyond a negative mentality into the realm of faith...for such a time as this?

The Mantle of Leading with the Heart: Joseph's Secret

As a young man Joseph led with his heart. He excitedly told his brothers of a dream and, unshaken by their lack of response, told them another. The problem was he had the starring role in the dreams and the brothers did not receive major billing. He was met with jealousy and resentment and although he was his father's favorite, his brothers had little use for him or his dreams. They hid him in a pit until they could unload him as a slave to a passing caravan. A bad situation got worse when he then landed in prison.

Amazingly, Joseph emerged from the pit and prison experiences still leading with his heart and equally important, without crippling bitterness over being wronged; his heart remained pure.

➔ **KEY**: Provide solutions while in prison.

Joseph was able to continue working in his spiritual gifts while in captivity. Having interpreted dreams for other prisoners, it is clear that Joseph had not retreated into himself when it would have been the natural thing to do. He didn't wait for things to get better before he became available to serve others. Rather than lose his spiritual vitality, he practiced his gifts in prison.

By being faithful in small opportunities, Joseph positioned himself to be called up suddenly. He built his resume as he went from pit dweller to slave to prisoner to keeper of the palace to man in charge of all food supplies in Egypt. He kept his heart equally unspoiled in times of humiliation and times of exaltation. Joseph was used mightily to minister to individuals while in prison and then to provide for the earth in hard times as the Prime Minister.

➔**KEY**: Keep your heart pure in good times and bad.

Many of us crater under intense personal trauma and never lay hold of the courage to look beyond our present problems. When Joseph literally could not see past his prison cell, did he recall the dreams in his heart as a young boy so vividly that he survived the pain? Did he find comfort in memories of the special coat of many colors his father had made for him? The way Joseph stewarded his heart and his life is an incredible example of one who did not allow the trials of life to get between a man and his God. He allowed God to provide for him spiritually before he became a provider for others.

➔**KEY**: A heart kept open towards God increases
your ability to hear God.

Abandonment did not destroy Joseph's life nor cause him to destroy the lives of others, unlike many of today's headline stories. Quite the opposite phenomenon appears as we watch this young man who traveled a horrific journey as a teenager somehow trade hurt and bitterness for service.

➔**KEY**: Trade your hurts for service.

He found hope wherever he ended up! Joseph remained alive spiritually because God provided a life-line for him, and he took it. God was Joseph's provider in every season.

➔ **KEY**: Grab hold of the life-line God extends.

Years later, when he again encountered his brothers who had betrayed him, we read of his intensely emotional yet spiritually mature response which reveals the man he had become:

> *[1] Then Joseph could not control himself before all those who stood by him, and he cried, "Have everyone go out from me." So there was no man with him when Joseph made himself known to his brothers. [2] He wept so loudly that the Egyptians heard it, and the household of Pharaoh heard of it. 3 Then Joseph said to his brothers, "I am Joseph! Is my father still alive?" But his brothers could not answer him, for they were dismayed at his presence. [4] Then Joseph said to his brothers, "Please come closer to me." And they came closer. And he said, "I am your brother Joseph, whom you sold into Egypt. [5] Now do not be grieved or angry with yourselves, because you sold me here, for God sent me before you to preserve life." (Gen. 45:1-5, NASB)*

Joseph's secret to leading with the heart was forgiveness which enabled him to hear God's voice. He refused to hold his brothers' actions against them and was therefore able to wield the great power God wanted to give him. Joseph was one idea away from becoming the most influential man in the world. Learning to hear God's voice positioned him perfectly to interpret the King's dream and advise him of an action plan for the world to survive the coming famine. Joseph created his own job description and was then asked to fill it. Many current day business executives are weighed down with unforgiveness and bitterness leading to a locked up heart unable to hear God.

Leadership Lessons for the Mantle of the Heart

1. Practice in prison. Become the go-to person for wise solutions. What solutions can you offer right where you are?

2. Forgive. Who must you forgive? Lead from the heart by forgiving someone for abandoning you or just not seeing you. Perhaps you were overlooked for a promotion. Perhaps you were betrayed by family and friends. When we forgive, we increase our capacity to love and become a solution even to the perpetrators of our pain.

3. Keep your heart ready and your gifts fresh. Joseph was working in his place when he was called up to interpret a dream for the king. As you provide solutions from a heart of forgiveness, you will be ready to minister suddenly when opportunities arise.

4. Arise and become the solution. It is time for the Josephs of the earth to rise above abandonment and become a vital connection to God, the source of our solutions in all arenas of life. Positions await creation by hearing from God and becoming the solution.

Pitfalls to Avoid: Retreating to Your Prison Cell

It has become popular to make a life story of your tragedy. While we need to acknowledge tragedy and the healing that comes, we also need to focus on where God has placed us and why. God is a master planner; there are places you will be able to enter and tools you will receive as a result of encountering the Lord in tragedy. These realities are positioning you to be of great help in your sphere of influence. Your tragedy and the resulting lessons give you credibility with certain audiences and spheres. What do you think you have been prepared to offer as a supplier of solutions?

The Mantle of Leading Leaders: Deborah

I look at the account of Deborah's integrated approach to life, work and ministry as one of the most complete and succinct examples of one who leads leaders. Picture Deborah the prophetess and judge going about her business in the house of Israel day in and day out. This mighty woman of God was positioned strategically for dramatic deployment into action. As Deborah performed her duties I doubt she ever dreamed she would call a king to war and ride a horse into battle – but she did.

➜ __KEY:__ If you sound the call, be willing to go.

In the account in Judges 4, Deborah called Barak forth and spoke to him words like this: "Barak, has not the Lord, the God of Israel, commanded you, 'Go gather your men'…" (Judg. 4:6 paraphrased). Barak was a leader of Israel. These words must have struck him as a startling reminder of something he already knew in his heart. So why did Deborah need to deliver the message? Perhaps it was because Barak was not acting upon his commission from the Lord. As the drama unfolded, Barak was encouraged to fulfill his God-ordained assignment to defeat Sisera, but not without demanding that Deborah ride into battle with him. In response she mounted up and cried, "I will go with you…" Many of us in this hour of cultural upheaval are looking for someone to go with us as well.

What kind of woman does such things? Who was Deborah?

Now Deborah, a prophetess, the wife of Lappidoth, was judging Israel at that time. She used to sit under the palm tree of Deborah between Ramah and Bethel in the hill country of

Ephraim; and the sons of Israel came up to her for judgment.
(Judg. 4:4-5, NASB)

We see immediately that Deborah flowed in spiritual ministry
as a prophetess, that her professional role was as a judge over
the nation, and that she was married. She also had a great
"office" with a view under a palm tree. We don't see any
hesitation in Deborah about moving in her spiritual gifts or
office as she performed her role as a judge. We see a woman
who had certainty and confidence in who she was in God,
and better yet, it seems she knew that God was in her.

➔ **KEY**: Know who you are in God.

Deborah didn't divide her life up into two tracks: The
Spiritual and The Professional. Granted, the culture Deborah
found herself in was an integrated one, unlike our western
culture that leads to compartmentalized living. Nevertheless,
Deborah didn't stop to say, "I can't prophesy today because I
am going to work – I have to sit on the bench under the palm
tree and render decisions and judgments. I'll follow up on this
at church when I see Barak. I'll call him aside to give him
God's reminder." No, not this woman!

She sent word to Barak, brought him into the office and
delivered the word with such confidence that it seems he was
compelled to issue an ultimatum that she come with him into
battle. Barak refused to go without her. Was it the strength in
Deborah's spirit that caused Barak to invite her to ride into
battle? What power we see in Deborah's words because her
life and her identity were firmly grounded in God.

Deborah was such a great leader because she understood her
assignment, she was confident in God's leadership and she
acted on her assignment in God's timing.

Because of her leadership, we read that those who followed were following with all their heart.

→ **KEY**: Understand the assignment and the timing.

The enemy got word of Barak's campaign and responded with "nine hundred chariots of iron." Barak may have been shaking in his boots or perhaps he was just waiting for the right moment to launch the attack – either way, once again it was Deborah who called the charge.

> *Then Deborah said to Barak, "Up! For this is the day in which the* LORD *has delivered Sisera into your hand. Has not the* LORD *gone out before you?" So Barak went down from Mount Tabor with ten thousand men following him. (Judg. 4:14)*

We see Deborah literally calling Barak "Up!" to go into battle. What was the protocol in the military? Who was in charge? God used Deborah, the prophetic judge and wife, as a military commander to bring victory in battle. All of Sisera's army fell by the edge of the sword – not a man was left.

What was Deborah's secret? How did she overcome the stigma of being a woman in office, flowing in the prophetic at work, leading in battle? Is it possible that Deborah flowed powerfully in these arenas of Family, Government and Religion, surmounting each challenge as though it was all in a day's work, because she was grounded in God? We tend to wrestle in our culture over moving between different cultural spheres. Deborah had her own struggles, but the answer in both time periods is the same: be rooted and grounded in the love of God so that He is the one we please above all else. We have given too much power to others to define us. Oh, that we too would run and live as Deborah did, with the primary goal of pleasing God.

➔**KEY**: Get deeply rooted and securely grounded in God.

Leadership Lessons in Leading Leaders

1. Engage spiritually as well as professionally. Because Deborah understood her professional and spiritual life as an individual, she was able to impact the government of Israel. Because of her leadership, Israel enjoyed a forty year period of peace.

2. Lead with confidence and passion. Incite joy in the ranks. Because of Deborah's leadership style, others gladly followed. Deborah's leadership was celebrated in a song recorded in Judges 5.

> *When leaders lead in Israel, when the people willingly offer themselves, bless the Lord! (Judg. 5:1)*

3. Lead in strength moving the heart. Deborah's leadership provoked others to search their hearts and make commitments. Judges 5:7b describes Deborah rising up as a mother in Israel. Whether she had her own children or not, I am not sure. But she had spiritual children in Israel who praised God and blessed the Lord because of her. Consider how you can motivate others with a leadership style that provokes a heart response. The leadership upon Deborah caused such commitment that we see references to "great resolves of heart" (5:15), "great searchings of heart" (5:16), and "people who jeopardized their lives to the point of death" (5:18). Leadership which gives glory to the Lord attracts followers who are willing to give themselves to a cause or a move of God.

4. Step up to the call. Deborah led a military leader and impacted a people group because she stepped up to

the call of God upon her life and her country. Look for opportunities to lead leaders into a greater expression of their mandates. Every leader needs a leader and few find them. Who do you know that could use a courageous call to action as Deborah gave to Barak?

➔ **KEY:** Encourage a leader to action.

Pitfalls to Avoid: Falling into a Typecast

As a Leader-Believer you can easily cave into peer pressure and take on a stereotypical role, adjusting your actions to meet the expectations of others by confining yourself to the "norm." Categories are limiting, so beware of conforming to society's expectations when you know God expects something else. You can easily overlook opportunities by assuming you have nothing to offer.

Resist the status quo and be willing to step out to lead other leaders. Don't disqualify yourself, but rather be willing to ask the question, "Hath God not said…?" Don't give the power to others in society to define your leadership. Rather, seek out identity from God Himself.

Your Custom Leadership Mantle

In conclusion, let's focus on your Custom Mantle of Leadership. Look through the recapped list which follows to choose the keys and lessons you will need in this season of leadership. Don't forget the traps, the pitfalls that await you. Arm yourself with a mantle to run long and run hard after God.

Recap of Keys, Leadership Lessons, and Pitfalls

Mantle of Authority: Elisha

KEYS:

➔ Go to Leadership School.
➔ Sign up hungry.
➔ Train by serving.
➔ Let the evidence speak.

Lessons:

1. Trust God for your leadership development.
2. Take the low road.
3. Remember, your development is a process.

Pitfall: Whining

Mantle of Marketplace and Worship: Lydia

KEYS:

➔ Be a worshiper of God.
➔ The Marketplace Mantle transfers to the ministry team.
➔ Develop your elevator speech.

Lessons:

1. Execute creative ideas to completion.
2. Bring work skills to the table.
3. Mind the home front.
4. Be a trusted team player

Pitfall: Making Excuses

Mantle of Daring: Daniel

KEYS:
→Dare to believe God for your identity despite the critics.
→Dare to rally praying friends. You need each other.
→Dare to look beyond yourself.

Lessons:
1. Set yourself apart to God.
2. Remain connected to friends, especially in adversity.
3. Hang on to who you are in God.

Pitfall: Giving Up

The Mantle of a Teachable and Resilient Spirit: Esther

KEYS:
→Pay attention to wise counsel.
→Respond to mentors if you want to grow past your affliction.
→Land on your feet; keep your footing.
→Carry yourself with a robust spirit.
→Frame yourself in the big picture.
→You may be God's strategy to reverse the enemy's plans.

Lessons:
1. Take good advice.
2. Come back quickly.
3. Get God's strategy.

Pitfall: Negative Mentality

The Mantle of Leading with the Heart: Joseph

KEYS:

➔ Provide solutions while in prison.

➔ Keep your heart pure in good times and bad.

➔ A heart kept open towards God increases your ability to hear God.

➔ Trade your hurts for service.

➔ Grab hold of the life-line God extends.

Lessons:
1. Practice in prison.
2. Forgive.
3. Keep your heart ready and your gifts fresh.
4. Arise and become the solution.

Pitfall: Retreating to Your Prison Cell

The Mantle of Leading Leaders: Deborah

KEYS:

➔ If you sound the call, be willing to go.

➔ Know who you are in God.

➔ Understand the assignment and the timing.

➔ Get deeply rooted and securely grounded in God.

➔ Encourage a leader to action.

Lessons:
1. Engage spiritually as well as professionally.
2. Lead with confidence and passion.
3. Lead in strength moving the heart.
4. Step up to the call.

Pitfall: Falling into a Typecast

Next Steps:

Now that you have identified specific components of your personal leadership mantle, give some thought to the questions that follow. Prepare to assemble your mantle by engaging with God about how to begin stepping in greater measure into your leadership reality. (Email info@7M-pact.com to request a template for developing your mantle and plan.)

1. How will you maintain a posture to know your God?
2. What is a specific assignment in this time and season where you can develop your leadership profile?
3. What skills and knowledge have you naturally attained by experience, training, or education?
4. What are some of the talents and gifts you have?
5. List 3-5 qualities from the mantles you have studied that you want to embrace as priority in your leadership profile for your current assignment.
6. Develop a 3-month plan (possibly projecting to a 1-3 year plan) to develop the qualities you listed in question 5 depending on how eager you are to grow in this season.
7. Compose your own prayer to *Engage with the Holy* for wisdom to develop your leadership and walk in humility.

Chapter 6
The How: Your Journey of Impact

Do you see what this means—all these pioneers who blazed the way,
all these veterans cheering us on? It means we'd better get on with it.
Strip down, start running—and never quit! No extra spiritual fat, no
parasitic sins. Keep your eyes on Jesus, who both began and finished
this race we're in. Study how he did it. Because he never lost sight of
where he was headed—that exhilarating finish in and with God—he
could put up with anything along the way: Cross, shame, whatever. And
now he's there, in the place of honor, right alongside God. When you find
yourselves flagging in your faith, go over that story again, item by item,
that long litany of hostility he plowed through. That will shoot adrenaline
into your souls! (Heb. 12:1-3, MSG)

PROPHETIC PROMISE – PRAYER – PREPARATION –
PERSISTENCE – POURING OUT

How many times have you longed to make a greater
difference, create a noticeable impact, or change what you are
doing in such a way that you will achieve a different result
than you have before – only to draw back because frankly it
just seems out of reach? How many times have you attended
a conference, been excited for forty-eight hours, and come
home ready to change your world until Monday morning,

when the alarm goes off, the inspiration fizzles and you go right back to business as usual? It is one thing to realize you were born to have an impact on your sphere of influence and it is quite another to be trained in how to reach that end.

I believe leaders are taught more than they are born. Are you willing to be taught? If yes, then embrace the concepts of this chapter and use them to set your pace and develop a life-stride powered by your awareness of the process by which Leader-Believers create impact. Honestly I am shocked by how little thought we give to the one life we have to live (until we get sick or reach the end of our years or sit at the graveside of another). People I know get more excited planning a cruise than they do planning their eternal homecoming!

→ **KEY**: Develop a life-stride for impact.

I wonder how Jesus felt when God spoke, rattling the heavens at His baptism, and said, "This is my beloved Son in whom I am well pleased." You and I are already His beloved sons and daughters through our salvation. He won't love us more for what we do, but wouldn't it be lovely to present a life well lived as our gift of affection and devotion to the Lord on the day we see Him face to face? Wouldn't that be wrapping it up with a bow? If I can delight my Lord by living full-out for Him, I intend to do it. Why wouldn't we live like this for the One we love? With that view in mind, let's look at what we can expect on the journey of impact.

Everything God has planned for you is within your reach with His help. You are not without a mentor, for Jesus is your way, your truth and your very life not only in salvation but in living out your salvation. I believe that if you keep your eyes on Jesus, listen to the Holy Spirit, remain teachable, refuse bitterness and take action on what the Lord shows you, then you can succeed in living your life well before God. Notice I did not say it would be easy or that everyone would like you. Leadership is not for the faint of heart. But for those who say "yes," "business as usual" is no more and the rewards are like gold.

→**KEY**: No more business as usual.

One of the success factors of every great leader I know personally is that they remain teachable; they are always learning. As you read on, don't analyze the information to see if you have ever read or heard it before. This is to ask the wrong question as a learner.

Have you ever told someone that you "work out all the time" when you haven't been to the gym in a couple months? Have you ever said, "Oh yes, I love to study the Word," when you haven't opened your Bible in weeks? It's not like you don't intend to work out and read the Word, but do you actually do these things?

The question that will move you forward is: "What *evidence* does my life provide that I am on track for impact as a Leader-Believer?"

A Track for the Journey

A track provides the pathway for a race car to travel to the finish line. We must define and travel the track to build our leadership skills; we need a master route. You can decide now how you want to shape the rest of your life, no matter what stage of life you find yourself in. You can greatly impact those around you, and this is worthy of serious consideration and prayer.

Regardless of whether you consider yourself an emerging leader or a seasoned executive, you have a current and future assignment to be fulfilled in the Lord. If you want to have a greater impact on those around you and in your sphere of influence, consider where you are going and how you will travel your journey to impact.

I have developed a list of 5 milestones that serve as a map for the journey. These milestones, the 5 P's, provide a route to our destination and define the track that will help us develop the character, beliefs and habits necessary to produce a lifestyle of impact as a Leader-Believer.

The 5 P's are:

1. Prophetic Promise – Vision for Your Life
2. Prayer – Engage with the Holy
3. Preparation – On the Job Training
4. Persistence – Stay the Course
5. Pouring Out in Power – Deliver Impact

1. Prophetic Promise: Vision for Your Life

Every destination begins with a vision of where you want to go; your prophetic promise is a vision for your life. The term "prophetic promise" simply refers to promises from God. Prophecy is called the testimony of Jesus (Rev. 19:10). In this context, we can say that prophetic promises reveal God's plans for us or His testimony about our lives, and this describes our destination in God.

The over-arching vision for your life is that you would know God's love for you, establishing the root of your identity in being loved by God (Psa. 139). Your journey in life has brought you to this place to understand how much God loves you. Within this vision of knowing God's love, you have a specific life calling to carry out assignments in your power alley. You might call this your vocation, such as being an entrepreneur, an artist, or a teacher.

➔**KEY**: Your over-arching vision and
your life calling are dynamically related.

It is usually within the context of our life calling that we realize the overarching vision of God's love and partnership, because we learn lessons best in the context of daily life and responsibilities. Just as sandpaper is used to get the rough edges off a plank of wood, our life calling proves to be the refining sandpaper of our souls.

Stewarding Prophetic Promise

As we go through life, God plants desires and prophetic promises in our hearts and lives in several different ways. Prophetic promises come to us through words of encouragement spoken to us by others, scriptures that stand out to us, dreams that we carry, or simply the desires God has planted in our hearts. A prophetic word edifies and inspires us in a mighty way. You need to weigh, pray over and consider the prophetic words you receive in order to ascertain the importance and place they deserve in your prophetic story line. This will enable you to stand the tests that come over time with a right perspective.

> *Delight yourself in the LORD;*
> *And He will give you the desires of your heart.*
> *Commit your way to the LORD,*
> *Trust also in Him, and He will do it. (Psa. 37:4-5, NASB)*

When we learn to discern the promises over our lives, we can enter into our responsibility or partnership with God to steward the promise. This is much like managing an investment or watering a garden. I developed a prophetic process inadvertently when I went on a beach retreat with two of my friends. We needed a getaway and, more importantly, were hungry to receive direction from the Lord about the course of our lives and critical next steps. We secured a beach-front condo in Galveston, Texas, and threw our things together for the trip rather spontaneously. As an afterthought, I grabbed some markers and flip chart paper. I never want to miss the opportunity to capture something exciting on a flip chart, just for the record.

As we arrived and settled in, we could hear the waves of the ocean rolling up on the shore, the sound of the seagulls calling, and we could taste the salt in the air. We munched, talked, laughed, relaxed, and began to sense that God was up to something strategic in our time together. We prayed and worshipped and by dark were ready to get down to the business we came to do with God. As we became increasingly aware that the Lord had orchestrated this very special time, we began to remind each other of different dreams and promises over our lives that we had heard each other speak about.

What unfolded over the next hours is now a process we use at regular intervals to review our life goals and prophetic promises. In this process we identified three areas of promise in each of our lives, celebrated evidence (no matter how small) that there was a measure of fulfillment, and then prayed into the future installment of what would happen to bring these promises into reality. Prophetic promises are a dynamic dimension of our spiritual lives rather than a stale mission statement hanging on the wall or an entry tucked away in a journal, as though there is no current activity. The process we used to steward our prophetic destinies was our way of asking God where we were on His timeline for these promises.

Capturing the times when the Holy Spirit moves upon you in terms of major life direction or calling will be key in journeying toward impact in the long run. I call these experiences or times "life marker events."

→**KEY**: Capture pivotal times, events, and prophetic
themes for future context.

*This charge I commit to you, son Timothy, according to the
prophecies previously made concerning you, that by them you
may wage the good warfare... (1 Tim. 1:18)*

The moving of the Holy Spirit, our Teacher and Comforter,
provides special times of comfort and guidance which we can
look back on when our promises are hotly contested or
beginning to fade. (My trip to Galveston, Texas, was one of
those times.) Every Leader-Believer goes through times of
training and testing and will wonder at some point, if not
many times, whether the promise of a significant life and
destiny was just a passing dream or the result of some rich
Mexican food. How we handle the promise over our lives will
be a determining factor in how we move forward.

Hope deferred makes the heart sick,
But desire fulfilled is a tree of life. (Prov. 13:12, NASB)

The writer of Proverbs acknowledges that hope put off, not
realized, results in a disillusioned heart. Our lives and careers
hold a certain promise over them that shapes our
expectations. The verse clearly likens our fulfilled
expectations to "a tree of life." The contrast of expectations
delayed or not met is the equivalent of hope deferred or put
off, which makes our hearts sick. Have you heard the
expression that someone was "heartsick" after a
major disappointment?

*Where there is no **vision**, the people perish...*
(Prov. 29:18a, KJV)

In this verse, vision can also be translated as "prophetic
revelation." Prophetic revelation, having our hearts touched
with the plans of God for our lives, is the fuel for keeping our

vision alive over time and warding off disappointment, disillusionment and "heartsickness." Scripture is full of powerful and great promises which sustain and motivate the development of any Leader-Believer who is willing to honor them, believe them and walk in them. I highly recommend finding a personal life verse and focusing on key scriptures for your spiritual development throughout your life, as well as becoming an experiential learner of the Bible.

Daniel 11:32b-33a is the passage I have taken for my life verse, encompassing all the expressions of my personal life, career and family. When I consider a new opportunity, I screen it through the lens of knowing God and taking action; this governs my decisions and choices about how to invest my time and energy. I rely heavily on Habakkuk 2:2-3 and 3:17-19 on a regular basis. What scriptures have stood out to you when you pray about your life vision and track? If you haven't identified a verse or two yet, take an evening to pray and search your Bible for a few encouraging passages to guide you in this season. Take hold of those for starters and know that God is able to add to it as you go. Developing the habit of going to God for encouragement in the Word is life to your heart now and in the future.

Over time, personal application by the power of the Holy Spirit takes these truths the short distance from your brain to your heart. Academic knowledge of the Bible is the basis for forming godly values and plans. We need both principles and heart knowledge to stay the course. When we know who we are to God and who He is to us, we can weather the most difficult of times. In fact it is in the difficult times where we sort out our faith and realize how much He loves us.

→ **KEY**: Major prophetic words will bring refining tests.

The Defining Value of Hard Tests

Joseph encountered many tests. He "had a dream" which stayed with him to be fulfilled much later in his life when his brothers truly bowed down to him as they came to collect grain during the famine. The dream from God and the coat of many colors from his father were prophetic promises deposited in his heart. But Joseph had to be thrown in the pit and learn to minister in prison before he reached the palace. The Psalmist wrote this of his experience:

> *Until the time that his word came to pass,*
> *The word of the LORD tested him. (Psa. 105:19)*

I have often said that big tests early in life may be the gift of God to establish faith. This was true for me as a teenager when I was injured in an explosion. A butane hot water heater blew up in our house when I was fourteen years old. I was severely injured with third degree burns which consumed the skin from my legs. I almost died that first night in the hospital; I could sense myself floating up off the bed. My Sunday School teacher, Evelyn Cochran, stayed by my side and had prayer chains going to ask God for my life. I had a long journey ahead of me in a burn center as the doctors planned skin grafts to place new skin on my legs.

> ➔ **KEY**: Your response to big tests early in life
> serves to establish your faith.

Although I had faced many challenges in my life by the age of fourteen, this was the place where God allowed me to define my faith. When I was suffering extreme pain, disoriented, sickened by the sight of my wounds, separated from my family members who were all undergoing their own treatments, and just surviving in strange surroundings, I had the opportunity to find out who God would be to me. I felt abandoned by God, yet I came to understand He had spared my life. As this sunk in, although my life was a shamble of painful bandage dressings, confusion, and many questions, I began to feel God's Spirit comforting me. I had no Bible, no teacher but the Holy Spirit Himself – and He was sufficient. We spoke of the *why*, the *where were You*, the hard questions. As we did, I realized I was conversing with the great Healer. I asked Him to heal my legs without the scheduled skin grafts. He did, day by day. This crisis of life proved to be the place where I would decide to believe God, no matter what the circumstances brought. I count the resulting knowledge of God's love for me in any circumstance as the most priceless gift, equipping me to thrive in life.

> → **KEY**: The hard times are the proving ground
> for the promises of God in our lives.

Many people go through life out of touch with how much God loves them, which makes everything else an uphill battle. We often are not able to see our own situation or progress in the heat of the battles of life. The value of having someone to speak truth over you when you cannot speak for yourself is huge. Sometimes the communion of the Holy Spirit helps you define your vision and establish a state of promise in your life. Sometimes He adds other people, like He did for me at the beach in Galveston that day. The importance of establishing your promise and vision in God cannot be overlooked. Look back at key times in your life to see who your God has become to you. This is how you create your history in God.

2. Prayer: Engage with the Holy

If our prophetic promise and vision describe our destination, then a life of prayer is the way we will travel. Road trips are the best for getting to know someone, with long hours to talk or ride in silence. My friend Michelle took me on a road trip to Kansas City that seemed to last for days – although it was actually one very long day. We talked, we laughed, we ate, we increased our faith during my driving and rested during hers, and we reached our destination closer than we were when we started out. Prayer is the essence of moving through the day in concert with God's breath and direction. At times it is a faint knowing He is guiding us. Other times it is urgent and deliberate. The daily life of prayer affords us road time with the Lord, engaging with the Holy.

Prayer is the reality of being in fellowship with God through all of our lives. Prayer is relating to the One who knew me before I was conceived, and prayer is relating to the One who sees me through my life and takes me to be with Him when I breathe my last breath. Prayer leaves no separation between me and my God.

No one thinks that a friendship or marriage or any kind of relationship will work, much less grow, if the two people involved do not engage in conversation. There are times that my husband and I have long talks over dinner about our lives, our family, our friends, and then there are times we communicate volumes with the glance of the eye. This can range from, "Don't you dare…" to, "Oh, there you are!" But the point is we are communicating in deep ways as we have grown in our relationship. Prayer is much like that. There are times when we meet the Lord and He draws us in, then we have long talks about the promises and the destination of the journey. At other times we receive the knowing glance from the One we love, yet we are learning all along to "pray without ceasing" (1 Thess. 5:17).

This pattern of prayer – engaging with the Holy – continues into our work lives. I have always relished mornings at home with the Lord, good coffee, a journal and an open Bible. We plan a day, consider strategy, and go back and forth over the affairs of the coming week. Prayer is a dance, a language, a convening of hearts and spirits, deep unto deep. There are times we are in so much pain we can only groan, then there are times we bombard Him with our lists. Other times it's questions. Most importantly, we know He hears and we learn to be still and know that He is God in times of prayer.

What happens when we pray?

God spoke the worlds into existence (Gen. 1), and we get to follow His example by speaking things into existence with our prayers. When we speak our prayers to God, not only for our own lives and families, but for our workplace atmosphere and coworkers, the Holy Spirit begins to move, to act. At creation the Holy Spirit was present in power, ready to move, but He waited until the Word was spoken. The same principle is true in our lives today. The power of the Holy Spirit is available when we pray in accordance with God's will. The angel told Daniel, "I set out to come at the sound of your prayer" (Dan. 9:23 paraphrased). I think of my prayer on a yellow tablet and the adventure the Lord answered me with, which affected not only my life and work in a major way, but the lives of many workplace individuals who came into a learning center bathed in prayer. The teams I hired, the lives that intertwined, and the boost to the economy of a county all flowed from a prayer I dared to write out during a workplace meeting. Just imagine for a moment what happens when we pray: hearts come alive, answers appear, people are healed and the kingdom is portrayed where we are…in the workplace.

Why must we pray?

There are things that simply will not happen if we do not lift our voices in prayer, in agreement with God's desires and in a longing cry for God to change a heart, change a situation, give wisdom, and simply be with us in our workplace role. Prayer is our tool to engage God's response and impact all spheres of society.[xxv] It is so simple (notice I didn't say easy…) that we often overlook it. As we pray we deal with the parasitic sins referenced in Hebrews 12:1-3. I have found that prayer for coworkers can change so much — my own attitude or another person's heart. I have literally experienced accusation against a coworker evaporating when I have actually stopped to pray for them (beforehand and in the moment).

How then should we pray?

There are many ways to pray and many tools to help us in our prayer lives. I find that my personal prayer life is the key to engaging with the Holy in all areas of life. A prayer list or prayer journal is a great way to record prayers and answers in our partnership with God.

Praying with one or two others goes beyond your personal prayer life; we find strength in praying with a group. Joining with others to pray about specific ideas or initiatives in our spheres of influence provides the opportunity to connect our prayers in the context of our relationships and our specific assignments.

Corporate prayer meetings bond us around a particular request for God's kingdom to come on earth as it is in heaven.

As we learn to pray in various settings, I think of a multidimensional approach that relates to our spheres of influence. I like to use an outline of prayer points that can apply personally and corporately.

Prayer Points for Bringing God's Presence in Your Workplace:

My vision and promise: Thank You for your promise over my life! Thank You for the way You are training me and walking with me. Thank You that I am called to my specific assignment. How can I know You better today, bring insight to others and take action in accordance with your direction for me?

My location, country, state and region: God, what are You doing in the earth? Breathe on Your plans for my specific area today?.

As we pray for nations, we remember our spheres of influence. Focused intercession for a region or a move of the Spirit takes prayer to another level as we look beyond our world of work. Prayer meetings for believers in the workplace all over the globe occur every Monday morning at the International House of Prayer in Kansas City. Believers from across the world join these prayer meetings on the internet, lifting up their requests to God. Our prayers help us realize our own smallness and our invitation to partner with the God of heaven in bringing His kingdom to earth.

My sphere of society: What specifically are You doing in my sphere of society? How can I bring God's presence in the realm of _____?

My sphere of authority: How would You have me lead others today? Who needs help, loving correction, guidance, vision?

My work: Lord, bless my company, the leaders, the teams, the customers. How can I bring Your presence today?

3. Preparation: On-the-Job Training

After we grasp the promise of a destination and adopt prayer as a standard mode of travel, we begin to realize that our path includes a long stretch of preparation. Preparation involves key on-the-job training experiences over time. As a leader works through these experiences, navigating plateaus and "in between times," there is a resulting growth or maturation in areas of skill, character, personality and responsiveness. Preparation spans many seasons in a life and is the place where most believers become disillusioned, disappointed, and lose sight of the bigger picture. A right understanding of preparation as a necessary part of the growth process helps us to appreciate these seasons as more than simply marching in place or even losing ground. Although it is exciting to learn new lessons, many of the lessons in this stretch involve painful learning. No pain, no gain.

Your Development is a Process

Dr. J. Robert Clinton of Fuller Seminary is responsible for developing Leadership Emergence Theory which outlines the stages of a leader's development. The stages include preparation and training, growth and testing, with the end goal of maturation.

Some will give great thought to this process while others will quite naturally move through these simple steps and phases of life. My dad was a simple man. He was raised as a poor farm boy and met God while working in the cornfield at age sixteen. Dad was guiding a plow behind two mules on the day God encountered him in the field as he pondered what would happen when he died. It seems a sermon about the saving power of the cross had grabbed hold of him at church and he realized he did not know Jesus as his Savior. He settled things in the field that day and later told us he let out a "whoop and a holler" as he danced through the field a saved man. Daddy never read a book like the one I'm writing here. God wrote the book on his heart and he lived it one day at a time by simply praying and following the leadings of the Lord. This simple yet profound way of living worked for my dad throughout his decades of service as a pastor and even in his last job serving as a Chic-Fil-A sample man. His humility and friendship with the Lord resulted in an incredible testimony.

I share this story with you because I don't want you to become overly analytical making a project of your life. Talk to God, pay attention, respond to the Lord, never quit, and whether you take a Ph. D. approach like that of Dr. Clinton or simply live like the farm boy Herbert Low, know that your goal is to finish well.

Because life in the workplace includes surprises and challenges, remaining unoffended at God and man is the ultimate challenge we all face with either approach. The partnership we have entered into requires that we continually communicate with God through hard times and unexplained delays so that we do not lose heart. The Lord is interested in each day of our journey of impact, not simply our arrival at the final stage of convergence. When we forget what the partnership is all about we may become overly fixated on the results or destination, finding ourselves irritated with God through the long stretch of preparation. Knowing that the preparation is a vital part of our journey relieves the pressure to "arrive" on time.

> *Blessed is he who does not take offense at Me.*
> *(Luke 7:23, NASB)*

Life GPS Helps

Keeping an eye on the final destination keeps us grounded while we travel the journey. When individuals are intentional about a life plan, this can grant perspective and stability in the process – because we all know there are ups and downs. Making some sense of them along the way and understanding that you are not the only one being subjected to the rigors of life development can ease the process along.

Of course each leader's timeline will look different and will be a picture of their individual life and choices. However, a few helpful general principles can be applied from the study of leadership. The stages identified by Clinton occur in every leader who perseveres whether the leader is aware of them or not. Being informed is powerful and helps a leader maximize the stages of development as outlined by Dr. Clinton:

1. Foundational development of an individual and their leadership potential
2. Inner life growth which involves testing
3. Maturing of ministry where gifts are identified and skills are developed resulting in the development of a person's life or ministry philosophy
4. Life maturing where a growing intimacy with God unfolds as God becomes a higher goal to attain than a life goal
5. Convergence when the leader comes to a point of maximum contribution
6. After Glow – bringing glory to God for a lifetime of leadership[xxvi]

The Destination is God Himself

At the end of a leadership life cycle we see the optimum phase of convergence which, unfortunately, few leaders press through to experience. Convergence is the guidance of the leader into a role and place of maximum contribution where the leader operates from a place of trust and rest, is content to wait on God and makes decisions toward convergence. The most fascinating part of arriving at this destination is that as God has worked in the leader over a lifetime and the leader has come to know God, the crowning jewel is God Himself—far surpassing the arrival at any key position or ministry goal. Yes the goals are attained, but they are no longer the main attraction.

> *The people who know their God...will do great exploits.*
> *(Dan. 11:32)*

This is a huge "Aha!" moment for leaders to aspire toward, aim for, and choose along the way. Otherwise, the journey can exhaust and spend the leader before they ever realize the ultimate reward of knowing God. Nonetheless, there is the awareness that God has placed within a leader a scope or sphere of influence for which he or she is responsible. It is every leader's goal to hear, "Well done, good and faithful servant."

4. Persistence: Stay the Course

A leader who knows the destination of their prophetic promise and remains connected with God during the journey will find the strength to finish well. Persistence requires initiative, follow-through, overcoming barriers, faithfulness in small things and a dogged refusal to give up. As we persist, we find we are building a history in God through all the seasons of our life. We begin to know more about how God speaks and that He may be silent for a season, and we develop the confidence that He is ever present and working.

There are many things that can derail a person from having impact. We are all too familiar with those who have settled for a secondary version of what might have been. I am not referring to a change of plans, or the need to make major adjustments along the way; I am referring to those who stop hoping in the Lord because He didn't show up as expected. When you *merely* expect God to be your vision fulfiller, you have taken a greatly distorted view of His role. On the other hand, trusting God to walk you into your destiny on His arm, through each surprise, each delight and each confusing circumstance, is saying to Him, "It's You and me no matter what the test or the journey may look like."

When my brother received his terminal diagnosis and I climbed up in the hospital bed beside him as we both began to cry, anything that had ever come between us before was now of no effect. Later, Dan said to me, "Lin, after that day, I decided it's you and me to the end…nothing will ever come between us again." When we allow life circumstances to come between us and the Lord, we have a major division in our souls and a house divided against itself cannot stand (Mark 3:25).

Persistence before God, pursuit of a close and growing relationship with your Maker, cultivating a dynamic prayer life – these are the things that will set you up to be able to stand the tests which refine you for the fulfillment of God's Word over your life.

➜ KEY: The Plan Changes but God Stays the Same

A pitfall to watch out for is attaching the plans of God in your heart to a very specific outcome that looks a certain way. Why? Because I promise it will not look like you think it will at the beginning. It is imperative that you are connected to the Lord and remain in an attitude of prayer and a posture of humility so He can mold you to fit His plans. Those who become rigid because of a fixed idea will encounter much heartbreak and disappointment. This misstep occurs when we become more attached to the *plan* than we are to the Lord. Under these circumstances there is an opportunity for course correction that most certainly will come because the Lord is not willing to be replaced by a plan in our lives. He wants to be in first place with each one of us. There was such a time in my life, which I now refer to as "the redbird season."

I had received a plan for my life from the Lord that involved a specific aspect of ministry, and I made a major life change in order to embrace it. Over time, it became clear that this plan was not working. I had left behind many things I loved and now found myself at a loss over what to do next. I had lost my bearings due to the disappointments and eventually, over a period of several years, began to release the dreams of my heart, believing I had been mistaken. Open handed before the Lord after prying my fingers off the dreams, I began again to sense Him drawing me in closer for a season of reflection. During this time I was in bed with a hip injury for several months. No longer could I busy myself with distractions; I was a captive audience before Him.

My husband was more than a little concerned to see how I would navigate through this identity crisis of sorts. He placed some lovely bird feeders up the hill so that I would see them from the bedroom window. Each day, Rick would open the curtains for me, turn on my favorite worship music, bring the coffee and allow me the time of reflection I so desperately needed. Over the days and weeks that followed, I felt as though the Lord took me by the hand through the disappointments of my life and held each one up for me to look at. It was as though I could hear Him say, "What about this? Do you think I didn't see you? Did you think I was not there? Don't you think I knew all about this?" And of course, situation by situation the Lord dissolved my pain as I felt His tenderness over my life. He corrected wrong beliefs I had allowed in my mind and began to relieve me of worries and cares.

The redbirds would come day after day, perch in the trees, then approach the feeders with wings spread to alight and feast – and entertain me day after day. The cardinals were adorned so beautifully, so bright against the tree bark and startling in the snow. Their display of beauty took me aback and I was thrilled to watch them feed and flutter. They were so carefree and I began to relish the days of worship and praise that filled these months as I received a joy beyond what I had experienced in years. In fact, I began to think that I would be happy to remain in the house, in this sweet state of communion for the rest of my life.

The hardest year of my life with two major surgeries, four months in bed, the loss of my dad and the loss of my brother, was also the year of the redbird season. I had lost much but gained more than I lost. I no longer looked for any major accomplishment to complete me; I was satisfied in Christ. This is our ultimate goal, to be so satisfied with Christ that every assignment and opportunity He gives us can be received with an open hand and an open heart. To know Him, to know our God, this is our identity which will overflow and enable us to accomplish great exploits. It is in this proven place that God begins to trust us with more assignments, the place when anything we do for Him and with Him will pale in comparison to our love for Him. Convergence brings things into perspective.

Whatever your redbird season might look like, decide now to stay in the dialog with God. Developing persistence requires that we stay in fellowship with God and a few trusted friends; this is our fuel to finish well. Be flexible when the plan changes and refuse to give up, and you will find yourself on course for the journey of impact.

➔**KEY**: Stay flexible to navigate changes well.

5. Pouring Out in Power: Deliver Impact

Pouring out what you have to offer in the lives of other individuals impacts your sphere of influence one person at a time in a powerful way. Some of you will impact entire nations and others will do the small stuff. The thing is, nothing is really that small. Every act of pouring out in power completed by Leader-Believers brings the presence of God and gives God glory.

Imagine for a moment that the millions of Christians in the world who are working and leading others got the reality that they were on holy assignment. Lives would be changed.

Many would want more of God as they experience anointed conversations, work success, and answers to problems. The church would be evident in increased measure throughout the spheres of society. The compounded effect of believers pouring out in power can change the world. Such living by men and women every day gives birth to a marketplace awakening.

When we pray for the opportunity and move out in simple obedience, God will meet us and show us how to pour out in power what He has deposited in us. You have invaluable skills you probably are discounting that would be like gold to someone else eager to learn. I take several young people a year through a process to create a map for their lives. I love doing it and have seen incredible results from getting people in touch with their dreams and God's plans and ways.

Many are without godly parents or examples and would eagerly welcome your leadership, your pouring out in power into their lives. The factor is not age, but willingness of heart to extend your life to touch another. It is never too early to begin pouring out as you go.

Examples could include a social media tech-type teaching responsible use of internet marketing, a city councilman hosting a prayer group for the city, a teacher showing young people how to make an outline or lesson plan, a philanthropist teaching how to build a foundation, a seasoned business leader teaching a young person how to begin a business...

> *For because of Him the whole body (the church, in all its various parts), closely joined and firmly knit together by the joints and ligaments with which it is supplied, when each part [with power adapted to its need] is working properly [in all its functions], grows to full maturity, building itself up in love. (Eph. 4:16, AMP)*

The whole body of Christ benefits when every joint supplies what it has to offer in the body of Christ. Many marketplace believers are dormant joints, not exercising their gifts in the workplace because they don't know that it is okay, that it is actually their job. The Scripture does not say that the body functions when the top pastors and TV evangelists do their work. It does not state that only some joints are capable of providing movement in the body, the effective work of the gospel, the completion of the work. It clearly says when EVERY joint supplies according to the effective working by which each part does its share; this causes growth in the body for the edifying of itself in love.

The body of Christ is to be closely knit, not disassembled into an array of parts. There is no room for a divide between the pastor and the banker, the priest and the teacher, the preacher and the mayor. We have become separated and the body is suffering. We must realign the body of Christ with every part doing its share. I am convinced we have many joints that are not contributing their part to the body of Christ because they have been misinformed. They think their ticket hasn't been stamped to be a Valid Joint. Well, this is your day. Consider Ephesians 4:16 the "stamp" on your ticket to contribute to the body of Christ by fully exercising your gifts and bringing impact where you are.

The journey of impact begins with a vision of the kind of life and influence you hope to create over the course of your developmental process in the workplace. This process must be bathed in prayer as you go, and there will be tests along the way. When you persist, keep talking with Jesus and stay the course, you will fulfill the promise throughout your life. You will pour out in power as you deliver impact by bringing God's presence to others. You will arrive full of confidence at your destination with a "well done" message from the Lord.

In celebration of your journey, no matter where you are, pray now for each milestone of the trip asking God to lead you to your final destination in Him.

Engage with the Holy

My Journey Of Impact

Dear Lord God,

Lord, thank You for calling me into a journey that I can finish well – to impact the world around me by Your design. I pray now for my response at each milestone of the trip.

Prophetic Promise: Thank you for promises from your word for my life. Lord bless those who have spoken promising words of vision in my life. Help me to wisely base my life vision upon sound direction from You that supports the vision to know and love you throughout my life.

Prayer: Help me engage with the Holy as my regular mode of operation, my modus operandi, that I might seek You, hear You, respond and know You in this journey You and I are on together.

Preparation: Give me understanding of the process of preparation as You give me the opportunity to learn of You through my work. Refine my character, teach me Your ways. May I understand the needs of those around me and be sensitive to Your Spirit as I discover You in the context of my work.

Persistence: Develop in me a tenacious spirit that won't give up. Give me strength to stay the course and learn from each time of testing and trial. Help me develop a perspective that remembers that You are working all things together for good.

Pouring Out in Power: Give me eyes to see where I can share what you have given me with those wanting to learn. May my life be an inspiration to those around me to go for it, go deeper in the Word, hunger and thirst for more of You, and desire to say yes to the partnership You hold out to us.

Finishing Well: Father, Give me awareness now, each and every day, to make the choices that will please You and allow me to travel well the journey of impact. On the day I meet You face to face, I pray You will say "well done."

In Jesus Name,

Signed:

Date:

AFTERWORD

What's Your Plan?

> *I'm not saying that I have this all together, that I have it made. But I am well on my way, reaching out for Christ, who has so wondrously reached out for me. Friends, don't get me wrong: By no means do I count myself an expert in all of this, but I've got my eye on the goal, where God is beckoning us onward—to Jesus. I'm off and running, and I'm not turning back. (Philippians 3:13-14, MSG)*

It is one thing to know you are meant to impact your sphere of influence with God's presence. It is quite another to actually do it.

Take a moment to recap your work:

☑ 1. Your Invitation: You have accepted the Invitation to Engage with the Holy at work. You are stepping into your identity as a Leader-Believer.

☑ 2. The What: You have settled the sacred/secular question. It's your job to bring God's presence into your workplace.

☑3. The Why: You are sure that you were made to Impact those around you.

☑ 4. The Where: You have explored your spheres of influence: location and time, society, and authority. You are developing a grid for how to bring influence and where.

☑ 5. Your Custom Leadership Mantle: You have customized your Leadership Mantle for this season and you have a development plan.

☑6. The How: You are on a Journey of Impact with milestones to mark your way: Prophetic Promise, Prayer, Preparation, Persistence, and Pouring Out in Power.

You are now ready to Deliver Impact.

Congratulations Leader-Believer…But there is a danger in reading this book.

It is to do <u>nothing</u> or to try to do it <u>alone</u>.

There is a simple solution:

Locate Your Inner Circle of 3: I challenge you now to make a short list of Leader-Believers you will share this journey with. Who comes to mind?

1.

2.

3.

Jesus changed the world through intentional interaction with 3 close friends, 12 team members to run with, and 70 others

He mobilized beyond that. It's a perfect strategy, but most people don't use this perfect God strategy.

After interacting with leaders at every level for more than three decades, my observation is that most ignore the powerful impact strategy of the 3 and the 12. As a result, they do not have the kind of lasting impact they were destined to deliver. That is a sad loss for these individuals and it affects those they *could have impacted* in ways we will never know.

Got my 3, what's next?

I have designed tools and processes to boost you to walk out your impact. It is called 7M-pact Community.

You will enjoy the 7M-Pact Community as your way to get fuel for your journey and grow in community. See which of these on-ramps best fits you now as a Leader-Believer:

____Emerging Leader-Believer: You may be a young person just emerging into your career or an adult who is rebooting.

____Established Leader-Believer: You are established in some measure of professional and kingdom living and you have been encouraged that you are on the right track and now you want to learn more and even get ready to take others with you.

____Executive Leader-Believer: You may have just realized what all your success has been unto and you are ready to focus your energies like a laser beam of influence guided by the hand of God.

Now it is Time to Take Your Place:

☐ 7. Go to 7M-pact.com

In the 7M-pact Community, you will find your on-ramp and discover templates, tools, and connections to walk out your unique Leader-Believer journey to impact.

I am not the only answer, but I am a very good one if you are looking for resources for the marketplace. Whether you are building from ground zero or plugging in now with your current teams, the 7M-pact Community will position you to run together alongside others who, like you, are ready to arise and shine.

I look forward to seeing you on the 7M-pact.com site and hearing how this book has Impacted you.

As you take your stand in the Marketplace Awakening, I applaud you in your impact journey. Jesus is so proud of you and I can just hear the great cloud of witnesses urging you to shine brightly in this hour.

> *Those who are wise shall shine*
> *Like the brightness of the firmament,*
> *And those who turn many to righteousness*
> *Like the stars forever and ever.*
> *(Daniel 12:3)*

Leader-Believers in the workplace,

This is your time to

Arise and Shine.

ABOUT THE AUTHOR

Linda Fields leads the marketplace ministry of the International House of Prayer in Kansas City. Prior to moving to Kansas City in 2007, Linda led a successful corporate learning organization in Texas, which positively impacted over 150,000 participants. While she finds her MBA, entrepreneurial experience, and university-level teaching beneficial, Linda credits prayer as the key to building a high performance organization which consistently delivered results with character, integrity, and love.

As an international conference speaker, Linda's passion is to release many men and women to impact their spheres of influence by stepping up as Leader-Believers, staying on course, and finishing well in their appointed destiny to know God and impact the world.

Linda specialized in communication post graduate studies at the University of Texas, earned an MBA and Bachelor of Science in Business Education from Texas State University. Linda and her husband, Rick, reside in the Kansas City area.

Linda's theme is to help men and women connect their personal destiny to a larger vision impacting their world. For more information on resources and events, please visit:

LindaFields.Biz
7M-pact.org

ENDNOTES

---

[i] Unless otherwise noted, all Scripture quotations are taken from the NKJV.

[ii] Timothy Keller with Katherine Leary Alsdorf, *Every Good Endeavor* (New York: Dutton, 2012), 48.

[iii] Jerram Barrs, 'Work: A Holy Calling,' *Knowing & Doing Newsletter* (Fall 2008), www.cslewisinstitute.org/webfm_send/461 (accessed June 3, 2013).

[iv] Darrow L. Miller quoted in *Business as Mission: Lausanne Occasional Paper No. 59*, ed. Mats Tunehag, Wayne McGee and Josie Plummer, (Pattaya, Thailand: Lausanne Committee for World Evangelization, 2005), 9.

[v] Timothy Keller with Katherine Leary Alsdorf, *Every Good Endeavor* (New York: Dutton, 2012), 19.

[vi] Jerram Barrs, 'Work: A Holy Calling,' *Knowing & Doing Newsletter* (Fall 2008), www.cslewisinstitute.org/webfm_send/461 (accessed June 3, 2013).

[vii] Jerram Barrs, 'Work: A Holy Calling,' *Knowing & Doing Newsletter* (Fall 2008), www.cslewisinstitute.org/webfm_send/461 (accessed June 3, 2013).

[viii] Charles Metteer, "A Survey of the Theology of Work," *Evangelical Review of Theology* 25, no. 2 (April 2001): 154-169.

[ix] *Business as Mission: Lausanne Occasional Paper No. 59*, ed. Mats Tunehag, Wayne McGee and Josie Plummer, (Pattaya, Thailand: Lausanne Committee for World Evangelization, 2005), 2.

[x] *Business as Mission: Lausanne Occasional Paper No. 59*, ed. Mats Tunehag, Wayne McGee and Josie Plummer, (Pattaya, Thailand: Lausanne Committee for World Evangelization, 2005), 6.

[xi] Charles Metteer, "A Survey of the Theology of Work," *Evangelical Review of Theology* 25, no. 2 (April 2001):154-169.

[xii] Mike Bickle with Deborah Hiebert, *The Seven Longings of the Human Heart* (Kansas City, MO: Forerunner Books, 2006), 6-7.

[xiii] Hugh Whelchel, *How Then Should We Work? Rediscovering the Biblical Doctrine of Work* (Bloomington, IN: Westbow Press, 2012), 8.

[xiv] Hugh Whelchel, *How Then Should We Work? Rediscovering the Biblical Doctrine of Work* (Bloomington, IN: Westbow Press, 2012), 8-11.

xv Hugh Whelchel, *How Then Should We Work? Rediscovering the Biblical Doctrine of Work* (Bloomington, IN: Westbow Press, 2012), 8-11.

xvi Linda Fields, *Find Your why Forward* (Mission KS: FIELD OF DREAMS PRESS, 2011), 60-74.

xvii Jerram Barrs, 'Work: A Holy Calling,' *Knowing & Doing Newsletter* (Fall 2008), www.cslewisinstitute.org/webfm_send/461 (accessed June 3, 2013).

xviii Loren Cunningham, "Transcript of Interview of Loren Cunningham on Original 7 Mountains Vision," Os Hillman, http://www.reclaim7mountains.com/apps/articles/default.asp?blogid=0&view=post&articleid=40087&fldKeywords=&fldAuthor=&fldTopic=0 (accessed June 13, 2013).

xix Hugh Whelchel, *How Then Should We Work? Rediscovering the Biblical Doctrine of Work* (Bloomington, IN: Westbow Press, 2012), 108.

xx Glad Heart Realty, "What Sets Us Apart?" www.gladheartrealty.com/apart.php (accessed June 2, 2013).

xxi James M. Kouzes and Barry Z. Posner, ed., *Christian Reflections on Leadership Challenge* (San Francisco: Jossey Bass, 2004), 120.

xxii *Merriam-Webster Thesaurus Online*, s.v. "influence," http://www.merriam-webster.com/thesaurus/influence (accessed June 18, 2013).

xxiii Matthew Henry, "1 Kings 19: The Call of Elisha," *Matthew Henry's Concise Commentary on the Bible*, Bible Gateway, http://www.biblegateway.com/resources/commentaries/Matthew-Henry/1Kgs/Call-Elisha (accessed June 20, 2013).

xxiv George E. Ladd, *Wycliffe Bible Commentary*, New Testament ed. by Everett F. Harrison (Chicago: Moody Press, 1990), 1154.

xxv Mike Bickle with Brian Kim, *7 Commitments of a Forerunner: A Sacred Charge to Press into God* (Kansas City: Forerunner Publishing, 2009), 36.

xxvi Dr. J. Robert Clinton, *Leadership Emergence Theory: A self-study manual for analyzing the development of a Christian leader* (CA: Printing Plus, 1989), 416.